Advance Praise for *Bugs for Breakfast*

"*Bugs for Breakfast* is at once a cookbook, a world tour of cultures, and an environmental exposé. Farts, feces, the Earth's future—Boone isn't afraid to go there. Middle-grade readers with a passion for saving the planet will gladly follow her through the *ew* and awesome of an eco-trend coming to a plate near you!"
—**Heather L. Montgomery**, author of *Bugs Don't Hug*

"Mary Boone's *Bugs for Breakfast* offers a fun and fascinating history of entomophagy, including the current global thought evolution happening around ways—and reasons why—to increase humans' use of insects as a food source. . . . This book will appeal to kids interested in world history, animals, fun facts, food and cooking, sustainability, climate change, and activism."
—**Lisa L. Owens**, author of *The Life Cycle of a Ladybug*

"Bugtastic!! This delectably comprehensive book is perfect for curious kids and adults. Full of history, environmental facts, recipes and even projects for kids, the reader will dive into the world of entomophagy and come away with a new outlook on what we see as food."
—**Ginny Mitchell**, Education Program Coordinator, Insect Zoo, Iowa State University

"*Bugs for Breakfast* is a f-ANT-astic blend of fun and facts that will inspire readers to not only #EatBugs but also think about how humans live on the planet and what improvements we can make for ourselves and others around the world. . . . *Bugs for Breakfast* is a tasty treat that goes well with everything from French flies to maggot-aroni and cheese to bee-ritos. Bug appetit!"
—**Rebecca Petruck**, author of *Boy Bites Bug*

"Young readers will gobble up this fascinating and informative book on entomophagy, the practice of eating insects. . . . Short, accessible, fact-filled chapters provide examples of dining on bugs in much of the world throughout human history, as well as detail the benefits and challenges of farming insects over other livestock. Want to conserve water, reduce carbon emissions, and feed an ever-growing human population? Then go for *Bugs for Breakfast*."

—**Mary Kay Carson**, author of *Wildlife Ranger Action Guide*

"Mary Boone's *Bugs for Breakfast* sparks curiosity and delights bug lovers of all ages in this well-researched and engaging book about edible insects. Readers will rethink squashing bugs and consider the ways insects as a food source can change our world."

—**Annette Whipple**, author of *Scurry! The Truth About Spiders*

BUGS *FOR* BREAKFAST

HOW EATING INSECTS COULD HELP SAVE THE PLANET

MARY BOONE

CHICAGO
REVIEW
PRESS

Copyright © 2022 by Mary Boone
All rights reserved
Published by Chicago Review Press Incorporated
814 North Franklin Street
Chicago, Illinois 60610
ISBN 978-1-64160-538-0

Library of Congress Control Number: 2021942200

Cover design: Sadie Teper
Interior design: Jonathan Hahn
Interior photos: Mary Boone
Illustration: Macy Ebright

Printed in the United States of America
5 4 3 2 1

For Mitch, Eve, and Eli, my greatest cheerleaders.

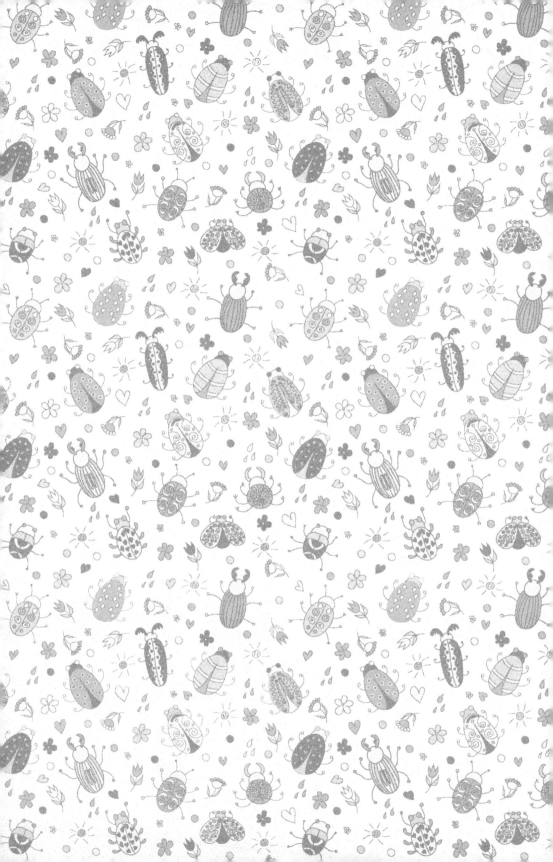

Contents

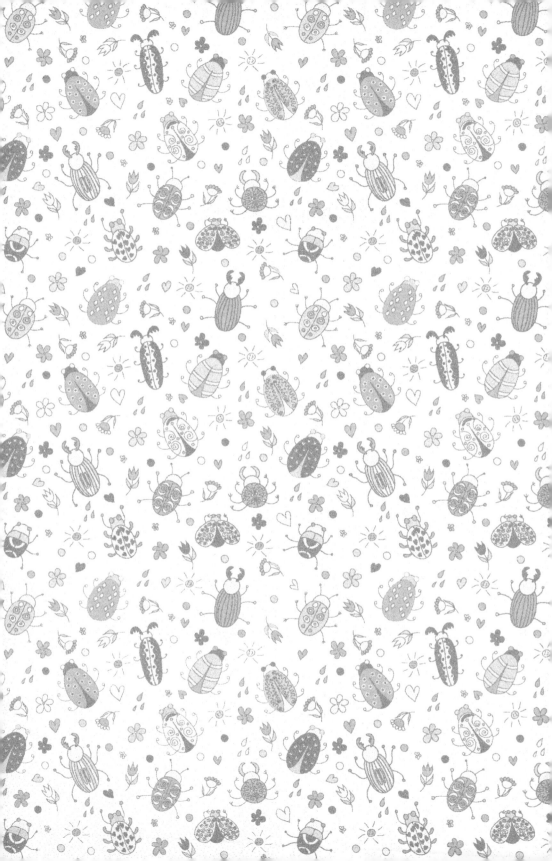

1

When Grub Really Is a Grub

The legs are the tricky part. Cricket legs tend to get stuck in your throat or under your tongue. And, seriously, who wants to go through the day with a cricket limb wedged between their front teeth? Not cool. So, pinch off the legs and start eating.

Crickets not your thing? Maybe you'll appreciate the nuttiness of roasted honeybee larvae. Black ants have a citrus taste, if that's more to your liking. Or how about giant water bugs? They taste like sweet crab meat.

This isn't a dare or some weird nature survival stunt. More than two billion people around the world regularly eat insects and arachnids. It is a practice called *entomophagy*, and it could be coming to a plate near you.

Entomophagy (pronounced en-tuh-MAHF-uh-jee) may sound crazy, but the truth is that people have been doing it for centuries. The word *entomophagy* comes from Greek: *entomon* means "insect," and *phagein* means "to eat." A person who eats insects is referred to as an entomophage.

Eating insects is mentioned several times in the Bible. John the Baptist famously lives on locusts and wild honey. The book of Leviticus even lists the insects that are OK to eat. Ancient Greek philosopher Aristotle wrote about feasting on cicadas, noting that the females were tastiest because they were filled with juicy eggs. More than 2,000 years ago, Ethiopians were using salt to preserve bugs so they could eat them when fresh ones weren't available. Around the same time, Nasamones, nomads from Libya, were gathering wingless locusts to dry in the sun and later pound into a fine powder. They mixed the powder with milk and drank it.

Most people use the words *insect* and *bug* to mean the same thing. Scientifically speaking, all bugs are insects, but not all insects are bugs. A bug is a type of insect. Bugs have mouths called stylets

Roasted crickets could spell the future.

that are shaped like straws, allowing them to suck liquid from plants or blood from other insects or people. Bugs also have thick front wings that are colored near their bodies and clear at the tips. If they have rear wings—not all bugs do—they're clear. Of the millions of insect species on earth, about 80,000 are "true bugs," including aphids, bed bugs, stink bugs, water bugs, and cicadas. Within the entomophagy community, the terms *bug* and *insect* are used interchangeably, and so this book will do the same.

The fact is, one out of every four people in the world eats bugs, insects, or arachnids. They're nutritious and delicious—plus, raising insects is more environmentally friendly than raising cattle or hogs. The Food and Agriculture Organization of the United Nations says eating more insects could help fight world hunger.

Entomophagy is practiced in most parts of the world, including Africa, Asia, Australia, Mexico, and South America. Beetles, caterpillars, ants, wasps, bees, grasshoppers, and locusts are the most commonly eaten insects, but they're hardly the only ones being devoured. In fact, more than 2,100 species of insects are regularly consumed in about 113 different countries.

So, why is it that in the United States, Canada, and Europe most folks would rather squish bugs than eat them?

Julie Lesnik, a professor at Wayne State University in Detroit, Michigan, studies the way the human diet has changed over time. She says being grossed out by a bug buffet is a cultural thing. "If you don't eat insects, it's probably because your parents, grandparents, and great-grandparents didn't eat insects," she says. In some societies, eating bugs was thought to be uncivilized; people associated insects with being dirty.[1] Somewhere along the way, a little kid in your family picked up a beetle or a caterpillar and—just as they were about to plop it in their mouth—someone yelled, "No! Don't eat that! Bugs are disgusting!" The words "bugs" and "disgusting" stuck in that child's mind. When she grew up, she told her children and grandchildren the very same thing. Then they told their children and grandchildren. And so, the cycle continued.

Many children in Thailand, Ghana, and Mexico grow up watching their friends and family eat bugs. So, those kids do the same—with zero disgust factor.

Professor Lesnik thinks that dining on dung beetles and gobbling grasshoppers will someday become commonplace in North America. But she says food trends take time to catch on. That's right, there are food trends—just like fashion trends and music trends. The foods we eat and how we eat them change over time.

Lobster, for instance, is now considered a delicacy, but it hasn't always been that way. When European settlers first reached North America, lobsters were so plentiful that piles of them washed ashore around Massachusetts Bay. Colonists considered them trash food, fit only for servants, children, prisoners, or the very poor. If times got hard and a family had to break down and eat lobster, they often buried the shells so others wouldn't know their dirty little secret. It wasn't until the mid-1800s, when trains began carrying canned lobster to stores away from the coast, that lobster's image began to change. For example, people in the Midwest developed a taste for canned lobster, but being far from the ocean, they had no access to the fresh meat. If they ever had the opportunity to travel to the coast, they ordered all the tasty fresh lobster they could eat. By the 1880s, the lobster's reputation had undergone a complete reversal. It was suddenly a delicacy, served only to upper-class folks. It's still considered fancy food. Today, a fresh three-pound lobster costs upward of $57.

Sushi is a more recent example. Fifty years ago, most Americans hadn't heard of the Japanese dish. Even if they had heard of it, the idea of eating raw fish and seaweed was unappealing to people who were used to eating hot dogs, steak, and TV dinners packaged in foil trays. Chefs tried some creative things to get diners to try sushi, including making rolls featuring ingredients Americans recognized. The California roll, made with cucumber, crab meat, avocado, and rice, was a good first step for those daring enough to try it. Before long, American diners became more adventurous.

Mealworm granola may be a good entrée into entomophagy.

They began sampling rolls made with eel, tuna, and squid—and they liked them. These days, there are about 4,000 sushi restaurants across the United States.

Lesnik thinks this same sort of thing could happen with insects. Diners may start by trying muffins, smoothies, cookies, or protein bars made with cricket powder. Before long, they'll step up to granola with mealworms or tacos made with grasshoppers. Eventually, people will begin to think of insects as tasty nourishment and the ick factor will disappear or, at the very least, it will lessen.

The US edible insect market has already seen small but steady growth, increasing in value from $6 million to $8 million from 2017 to 2018. You still won't find edible insects in most North American supermarkets, but that may change soon. Worldwide, experts believe the edible insect market will grow to more than $4.6 billion by 2027.

Athletes, many of whom are knowledgeable of the ways in which nutrition affects performance, have helped build awareness. Ten-time NBA All-Star Carmelo Anthony, Major League Baseball pitcher Mark Melancon, six-time Ironman triathlon champion Jordan Rapp, and Olympic triathlete Kathy Tremblay are among those who include protein-rich insect-based products in their diets.

Celebrities are doing their part to shine a spotlight on the subject. Actors Zac Efron, Nicole Kidman, Salma Hayek, and Angelina Jolie have all spoken publicly about the ways in which they incorporate insects into their diets. Singer Justin Timberlake served grasshoppers and ants coated in black garlic and rose oil at the 2018 launch party for his album *Man of the Woods*. American rapper Nas invested in Exo, a company that makes protein bars from cricket flour. And actor Shailene Woodley, who has eaten both ants and June bugs, says, "I think the future of food is insects."[2]

Environmentalists, too, are leading the way in educating the public about entomophagy. It takes less space and fewer resources to raise crickets or mealworms than it does to raise beef cattle, hogs, or chickens. In addition, more and more North American universities, colleges, and independent researchers are investigating entomophagy. They are studying topics ranging from food safety and recipe development to consumer perceptions and regulatory challenges faced by the industry.

Ready to join the entomophagy movement?

Step one is to become informed. Becoming an entomophage is not as simple as gathering a bunch of bugs from your yard or garage and eating them. For starters, there are more than two million different types of insects in the world. About 900,000 of those insect species have been identified and named, but only 2,100 have been found safe to eat. Some bugs may upset your stomach, and many species simply haven't yet been tested. Allergies are another concern. Insects have exoskeletons that support and protect their bodies, similar to the exoskeletons in crustaceans such as crabs, lobsters, and shrimp. So, it makes sense that some people with shellfish allergies also are allergic to insects. It's also important to understand that different bugs have different flavors, so it often takes some experimenting to figure out which species appeals to your specific palate.

Before you eat any insect, you also need to know how it lived and died. A bug you find in your basement or in the wild may be infected with microscopic parasites, or it could have been sprayed with poisonous chemicals. The insects that are served in restaurants or made into protein powders or bars have been grown in safe, sanitary environments.

Eating insects does not require bravery, but you must have an open mind and a willingness to try new things. Sound like you? Keep reading!

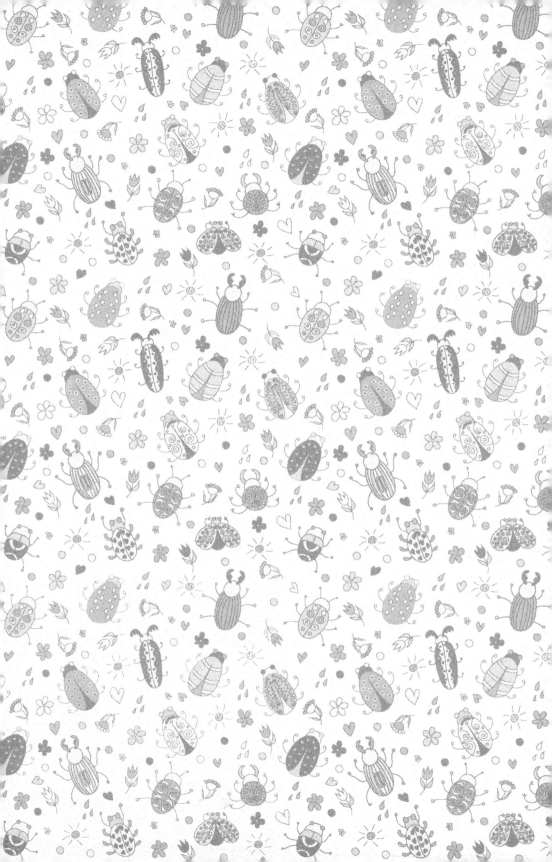

2

Crickets, Bees, and Ants, Oh My

One hundred thousand years ago there were no grocery stores, deli counters, fast-food restaurants, or shops boasting 31 flavors of ice cream. Early humans collected birds' eggs, berries, and wild greens. They speared fish, and hunted animals such as buffalo, antelope, and wild goats. They also ate bugs.

By analyzing artifacts, archaeologists have determined that *Homo erectus*, the ancient ancestors of modern humans, began eating insects several million years ago. Hunting was difficult. When no prey was found, they often scavenged for meat off carcasses left behind by other animals. Gathering insects was both less dangerous and more reliable than hunting. This was important because women, who generally stayed home while men were hunting, were able to safely collect ants or dig for termites while caring for their young children. When hunters returned with little or no bounty, families were not doomed to starvation. They could fry up some flying termites or make a stew of mopane worms to get the nourishment they needed.

Today, in much of the Western world—specifically the United States, Canada, and Europe—insects are considered the food of the future. Some of this is due to the fact that colder climates don't support the variety of insects found in tropical climates, causing human-insect interactions to be rarer, historically. But for more than 80 percent of the world's population, insects have been an important part of their diets for centuries.

Which insects people are eating and how they're eating them depends largely upon where they live. Here's a quick overview.

AFRICA

According to the Food Aid Foundation, approximately 795 million people in the world do not have enough food to lead a healthy, active life. That means hunger affects one out of every nine people on earth. Sub-Saharan Africa is the region with the highest percentage of its population suffering from hunger. One of every four people there is undernourished. Insects are often the only way to fight off starvation.

Insects have been eaten in Africa for thousands, maybe even millions, of years. The continent is home to more than 500 species of edible insects, ranging from caterpillars and termites to bees and beetles. In some regions, especially those battling intense heat and drought, insects are the most consistent food source. In the Democratic Republic of the Congo, for example, insect consumption among members of the Gbaya tribe accounts for up to 20 percent of their protein intake. Harvesting, processing, and selling insects contribute to many families' incomes. A large handful of boiled and salted caterpillars sells for the equivalent of $1.20.

In southern Zimbabwe, women and children often collect mopane worms. Depending upon where in Africa you are, these worms are also known as madora, phane, amacimbi, mashonja, or omagungu. Mopane worms get their English name because they eat the leaves of the mopane tree. Mopane worms are big—as long as your hand and as fat as a cigar. To harvest them, the worms are gathered by hand, plucked right off the trees. Their bright green, slimy guts are squeezed out and the outsides of the worms are smoked or laid out to dry in the hot sun. When dry, the worms turn a chalky gray color. Dried mopane can be eaten plain, as a crunchy snack, or they can be cooked in a spicy stew and served with cornmeal porridge.

Mopane worms also are popular in northeastern South Africa, as are stink bugs, grasshoppers, locusts, and termites. Termites here build huge mounds, towering 15 feet (4.5 m) or higher. Termite hunters, often elderly women in a village, use pickaxes to bust through a mound's thick exterior wall. They then spit on reeds and insert them into the mound through the holes. Termites inside the mound will try to fight off the attacking reed and jump onto it. Bad choice. The hunters quickly pull the reeds from the mound and brush the accompanying termites into buckets. This process is repeated until enough termites are harvested to eat or sell. A 2018 study conducted by researchers from the University of Witwatersrand in Johannesburg found that termites are important both for the nutrition and income they provide to many poor South Africans. One kilogram of termites (2.2 pounds) sells for 100 rand (about $5.92). That may not sound like much, but in 2015 more than 30.4 million South Africans—55 percent of the population—were earning less than 992 rand (about $75) per person per month.

Entomophagy also is practiced in parts of Cameroon, the Central African Republic, Congo, Nigeria, Uganda, and Zambia.

ASIA

The world's top three insect-eating countries are all located in Asia: Thailand, Vietnam, and China. You won't exactly find crickets on the menu at McDonald's restaurants here, but it is common to see carts in Bangkok's night markets or Phuket's Naka Market piled high with deep-fried insects and impressive-looking bug kabobs. One of Thailand's most popular snacks is *jing leed*, deep-fried

Kabob made of roasted grasshoppers and silkworms.

crickets seasoned with Golden Mountain sauce (similar to soy sauce) and Thai pepper powder.

In parts of Vietnam, a stir-fry dish called *nhong* is popular. It is made with silkworms, scallions, and a splash of fish sauce. The Vietnamese also enjoy fried cicada, bee larvae, and scorpion. *Xoi trung kien*, sticky rice mixed with seasoned ant eggs, is a traditional dish of the Tay people in the northern mountains of Vietnam.

Canned baby bees, silkworms, and grasshoppers are sold at Japanese markets and often eaten cold, straight out of the tin containers. A relatively new sight in Osaka and Tokyo, two of Japan's largest cities, are insect vending machines offering packets of zebra tarantula, chocolate-coated grasshoppers, and rhinoceros beetles. A dish called *inago* features fried locusts cooked with soy sauce and sugar; the dish is popular in Japan's mountain regions.

Insects have been eaten in China for more than 2,000 years. Because of this, many researchers have focused on the country's rich bug-eating culture. In 2017, the Institute of Zoology at the Chinese Academy of Sciences found that 324 species of insects were either being eaten in China or used for some sort of medicinal purposes. Just 10 to 20 types of those insects are eaten on a regular basis, including grasshoppers, silkworm pupae, wasps, bamboo worms, and stink bugs. Fried or roasted cicadas are one of the country's most popular insect snacks.

In northeast India, entomophagy is practiced by many tribal communities, with consumption varying greatly by tribe. Members of the Nyishi tribe, for example, like stink bugs and white grubs, while neighboring Galo tribesmen tend to prefer wasps. Both tribes consume short-horned grasshoppers and crickets.

In Indonesia it is fairly common to be served dishes made with bee larvae. Bee brood, which looks like honeycomb but is filled with larvae, is gathered and then boiled to get the larvae out. It is often mixed with chopped tomatoes and chili peppers, wrapped in banana leaves, and steamed to create *botok tawon*, a spicy dish eaten with rice.

Cambodians also love their insects. Crowded markets are filled with vendors selling fried crickets and roasted ants. Many children snack on maggots fried with chilies and spring onions. Super-crunchy deep-fried tarantulas are a treat, hairy legs and all.

AUSTRALIA

The role insects played in the diets of the Australian Aboriginal people before the arrival of European settlers varied greatly, depending upon both the availability of edible insects and other plants and animals. Many historians believe the Aboriginal people primarily ate insects to supplement their diets. They consumed bogong moths for their fat and ate honey ants and sugarbag bees to add sweetness to their foods.

In recent years there have been efforts by some chefs to develop entrées based on traditional indigenous foods. For example, green ants, also known as weaver ants, can be found across northern Australia. The ants were traditionally used as medicine but have become sought-after ingredients. Top-tier chefs are adding them to everything from fancy cheeses to mango desserts. The insects are in such high demand, they're now selling for approximately $228 per pound (.45 kg).

Circle Harvest, Australia's largest and oldest bug farm, got its start in 2007 under the name Edible Bug Shop. Its founder, Skye Blackburn, is an entomologist and food scientist. She has become a world authority on insect-farming techniques and is at the forefront of developing edible insect products. Additional meal worm and cricket farms have popped up in recent years, but insects are still very much a niche market in Australia.

CENTRAL AMERICA AND SOUTH AMERICA

Brazil, Colombia, Venezuela, Ecuador, and Peru are top insect-eating countries in this region. Which insects are eaten varies according to history and tradition. Beetles, bees, wasps, ants, butterflies, moths, and termites are among this region's most popular edible insects. They may be eaten raw, roasted, wrapped in leaves and steamed, fried, baked, or smoked.

The Santander region in northern Colombia is famous for its seasonal insect treat *hormigas culonas*, which translates to "big-bottomed ants." Harvested in the spring, these ants have bulging butts and are most often roasted, salted, and eaten like popcorn.

In Peru waykjuiro worms are gathered and roasted. The small orange and black worms make a crunchy snack any time of the day but are often enjoyed with breakfast. Larvae of the palm weevil, known as *suri*, are staples of the Amazonian diet. The fatty grubs can be fried, roasted, or barbecued on a spit.

In Brazil, queen ants, or *icas*, are a delicacy. They are traditionally eaten in October and November, when thunderous rains force them out of the ground. Icas are fat and can grow up to an inch long. They can be cooked or eaten raw. Those who choose to eat them alive rip off the insects' lower jaws so they don't get bitten while they chew. Icas have become scarce in recent years because of pesticides used to protect trees grown for paper production.

EUROPE

Europeans have a well-documented history of eating insects, dating all the way back to ancient Rome and Greece. The scholar Pliny wrote that royalty and other wealthy Romans enjoyed eating beetle larvae that had been raised eating flour and wine. Still, in recent centuries, Europeans have largely turned up their noses at the idea of dining on bugs.

In January 2021, the European Food Safety Authority OK'd the use of dried yellow mealworms for human consumption. The agency may soon offer similar approval for crickets and grasshoppers. Insects are already available for human consumption in a small number of European countries and are more widely produced for use in animal feed.

Experts predict that once approvals are granted, the European market for insect-based food powders, bars, breads, and such will grow quickly. Economists predict that by 2023 Europe will become the world's second-largest edible insect market, trailing only the Asia-Pacific region. By 2030, it is expected that Europeans will be buying and consuming more than 286,000 US tons (260,000 metric tons) of insect-based foods each year.

MEXICO

Eating insects is an important part of Mexico's history. In small villages and rural areas, many of these traditions live on. City diners, however, largely gave up their bug-eating ways—until recently, when some of the country's top chefs began creating trendy and delectable insect-based dishes.

Quintonil is a restaurant located in Mexico City. It has a reputation for fine dining. In fact, it has been voted one of the 50 best restaurants in the world. What are people flocking to this fancy restaurant to eat? Innovative dishes such as chicatana chorizo sausage, made with chicatana flying ants and fresh fish served in a stew made of grasshoppers and beans.

Chefs at other high-end Mexican restaurants have also created buggy menu items. Escamol is ant pupae and larvae that's been fried with butter, onions, and chili; it's often called "Mexican caviar" and is considered a delicacy. It's also not difficult to find ant-infused mayonnaise, crunchy grasshoppers mixed into guacamole, or omelets dotted with roasted ants.

Chapulines, grasshoppers that have been roasted and seasoned with chile powder and lime, have been a Mexican specialty for hundreds of years. They can be eaten as a snack or served in tacos in place of meat.

MIDDLE EAST

In the eighth century BC rulers in the Neo-Assyrian Empire impressed their guests by having maids serve oversized locust kabobs at royal banquets. Flash forward about 2,800 years to 2014, when the world's first commercial grasshopper farm was opened in

Israel. Founder Dror Tamir named his company Hargol, after the kosher grasshopper from the Bible. The company has centered its business around creating grasshopper protein powder that can be added to shakes, energy bars, pasta sauce, and baked goods. Hargol is a high-tech farm that sells its products worldwide.

Locust swarms covering several hundred square miles have threatened Yemen and Saudi Arabia in recent years. The Food and Agriculture Organization of the United Nations reports that a small swarm of locusts can devour the same amount of food that would be eaten by 35,000 people. When locusts arrived in Yemen in 2019, villagers took advantage of the swarms by using them as an alternative food source. Villagers caught the locusts at night, when they weren't flying, by throwing scarves over them to trap them. They then swept them into bags using shovels or their hands. "Instead of them eating our vegetables, we now eat locusts with rice and our vegetables are fine," a local farmer told the *Middle East Eye* newspaper.[3]

Yemenis have long faced a food crisis. But in Middle Eastern countries where hunger is not as common, eating insects is still a novelty.

NORTH AMERICA

Across North America a large variety of insects was consumed as traditional food by some natives and settlers.

Historians believe that Native Americans ate as many as 90 different species of insects. For example, the Northern Paiute lived near Mono Lake in what is now eastern California. Shore flies, also known as brine flies, live most of their lives in the water. The Northern Paiute collected fly pupae by the basketful from the shallow water along the shoreline. The pupae could be dried, eaten raw, fried, or ground into a powder for use in breads and cakes.

Cherokee in North Carolina dug up young cicadas and fried them in animal fat. Members of the Tlicho tribe, located in Canada's Northwest Territories, ate gadfly larvae. According to historians, the larvae were plucked from the skin and tongues of hunted caribou and were eaten raw. And the Goshute, who lived in present-day Utah, were so accustomed to eating grasshoppers, locusts, and crickets that, when they first tasted shrimp, they are reported to have called the creatures "sea crickets."

European settlers, though not as daring, also ate the occasional insect. The Ute, a tribe that lived in the region that is now Utah, harvested katydids, which they ground into powder, and baked into high-protein, high-calorie snacks called prairie cakes. When the crops of neighboring European settlers failed and they were on the brink of starvation, the Utes sold them prairie cakes. The hungry Europeans reportedly found them to be tasty.

As more sophisticated tools and stable food sources became available, both Native Americans and European settlers gave up their bug-eating ways.

In recent years, some Native American tribes have tried reintroducing the practice to pay tribute to their pasts. Others have taken an interest in eating insects because of growing demand for sustainable high-protein foods.

By fall 2020, somewhere between 150 to 300 edible insect farms had sprung up across the United States, most of those so small they produced just enough insects to serve one or two local clients. There were a handful of larger farms in North America, but they certainly were not the norm. Cricket protein and protein bars had found their way onto the shelves of several regional retailers and health food stores, and whole roasted crickets and mealworms were available at countless farmers' markets and through the Internet. Thanks to a growing demand for environmentally friendly and high-protein diets, the sale of edible insects within North America is expected to outpace all other regions from 2020 to 2027.

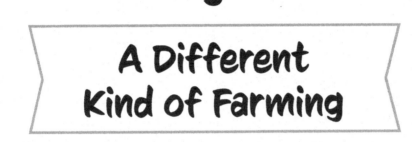

3

A Different Kind of Farming

Cows are big animals. The average mature beef cow tips the scales at around 1,200 pounds (544 kg)—that is heavier than a concert grand piano. It takes some serious space to raise an animal that large. The US Department of Agriculture recommends at least 20 to 30 square feet (6 to 9 m) of barn space. Plus, you'll need one acre (a little smaller than an American football field) of pasture per cow, so they can graze and move around. It takes about 18 months to raise a beef calf to maturity, and that 1,200-pound steer will yield about 490 pounds (222 kg) of boneless, trimmed beef.

In that same one-acre space and over that same time period, you could raise roughly 1.3 billion crickets. That's approximately 1.3 million pounds (590 million kg) of edible cricket protein.

Why does any of that matter? Because by 2050 experts predict that the world's population will grow to nearly 10 billion and current food production will need to double to feed all those people.

In 2019, researchers at the US Geological Survey used satellite imagery to determine that there were about 4.62 billion acres (187 billion ha) of farmland worldwide. Many scientists worry that erosion, overuse, and chemicals are reducing the amount of available high-quality farmland. Doubling the world's food production might not require twice as much land, but it would definitely require more farmland than we currently have to raise two times the beef cattle, two times the hogs, two times the chickens, two times the wheat—well, you get the idea. More people will be eating more food that will have to come from less land. Even if space weren't an issue, the expense and environmental impact associated with traditional livestock farming raises big concerns for those trying to figure out how to feed the world's growing population.

Many scientists believe insect farming could be a wise alternative. Edible insects require less feed and far, far less space than traditional livestock. It takes 25 pounds (11.3 kg) of feed to produce one pound (0.45 kg) of beef, and only two pounds (0.9 kg) of feed to produce one pound of crickets. When you factor in irrigation of the grains and grasses in feed, plus water for drinking and processing, one pound of beef—that's four fast-food burgers—requires about 1,800 gallons (6,814 l) of water. Whereas growing a pound of crickets (about 1,000) takes just one gallon (3.8 l) of water.

It's true that people in many parts of the world have been eating insects for centuries, but insects in many of those places are caught wild, rather than farmed. An exception to that rule is Thailand, where 20,000 cricket farms produce a combined 7,500 tons (6,800 metric tonnes) of crickets per year. The country leads the world in insect production and exportation, supplying insects to many European and North American processors.

While entomophagy is just beginning to make inroads in the West, US farmers have been raising crickets to feed to fish, reptiles, and pet spiders for more than 70 years. Raising crickets for humans to eat, though, is relatively new.

If the idea of cricket farming conjures up visions of teeny-weeny tractors plowing itsy-bitsy fields, think again. Most cricket farms look more like warehouses than traditional farms, and they are often located in industrial areas rather than the rolling countryside. The largest "farms" are set up in sterile-looking buildings stacked high with metal shelving and thousands of bins filled with crickets. They use robotic systems to deliver feed and water directly to each bin. Workers check computer screens to monitor the food intake and life stage of the insects in each bin. Sensors throughout the facilities work around the clock to record information about temperature, humidity, and oxygen levels. Alerts are set so workers can immediately respond if something goes wrong.

Smaller cricket farms are popping up in garages, barns, and even office buildings, where insect care is much more of a hands-on activity.

While many types of insects can be raised as food, crickets are most often eaten and farmed in North America for several reasons. For starters, they are considered "the gateway" bug for those new to entomophagy. They're not too big or scary looking. Their taste is fairly neutral. They can be ground up for use as protein powder. They're also easy to raise.

There are approximately 900 species of crickets in the world, but *Acheta domesticus*, commonly called the house cricket, is most often farmed. These yellow to light-brown crickets generally grow about three-quarters of an inch long. The *Gryllodes sigillatus*, also known as the tropical banded cricket, is slightly smaller. It is less popular but has also found its way into some cricket-growing operations.

Because insect farming is a relatively new concept, those getting into the business often find themselves experimenting to come up with the best equipment and processes. Talk to anyone who has tried their hand at raising crickets, and you'll hear frustration about the many things no one told them. Cattle, hog, or chicken farmers can learn tricks of the trade by reading books, magazines, or websites. They join industry associations or enroll in agriculture-related courses in high school or college. For insect farmers, those resources are difficult to come by.

Shelby Smith, a 30-year-old from Iowa, left a career in finance to raise crickets in her home state. "My dad's been a farmer most of his life," she says. "When I came home to work on the family farm, he told me he hoped I didn't battle the same corn and soybean markets he'd been fighting for 30 years. His advice was to find a niche and go for it. I'm pretty sure he was thinking I'd choose something like sugar beets or grass-fed beef. I don't think he ever dreamed I'd become a cricket farmer."[4]

Farmer Shelby Smith stands amidst the bins in her "Cricket Castle."

In January 2018, Smith began working to streamline a cricket growing operation that can be housed in a retrofitted single-wide trailer—she calls it her "Cricket Castle." She wanted to create a cricket-raising environment that could be easily replicated so she could get other farmers to raise crickets for her. Bins filled with crickets are numbered and detailed records are kept. Through trial and error, she has learned the best size and style of bins to use, how to make those bins escape-proof, and the best ways to ventilate both the bins and the trailer. She's invested in extra insulation and high-powered heaters because crickets prefer temperatures between 80 and 90 degrees Fahrenheit (26°C to 32°C), which can be really hard to maintain during Iowa's brutally cold winters. She's also learned how to water the insects without drowning them.

That's right. Baby crickets can drown in even a drop of water. Crickets and other insects take oxygen in through openings on the sides of their bodies called spiracles. Put a bowl of water in a cricket bin and they'll hop in for a drink—and drown.

"The ventilation, the temperature, the watering . . . I probably killed a million crickets trying to get everything just right," says Smith. Now she uses raw potatoes cut into quarters to water the babies, called nymphs or pinheads. The tiny insects can safely suck moisture out of the vegetables. She uses baby chick waterers for more mature insects but fills the bases with small stones so crickets can perch on the rocks while hydrating.

Diseases, such as Cricket paralysis virus (CrPV) and *Acheta domesticus* densovirus (AdDNV) are another threat to insect farmers and their flocks. In 2010, AdDNV killed millions of crickets that were being raised to feed zoo animals and pet reptiles. The disease killed 60 million crickets in ten days at Krickets Un, a farm in Lacombe, Alberta, Canada; that farm is no longer in business. Michigan-based Top Hat Cricket Farm was selling 5.5 million to 6 million crickets per week when the virus wiped out its entire farm. It has since rebuilt its business and is raising and selling the more disease-resistant *Gryllodes sigillatus* species.

Crickets are omnivores, which means they eat both plants and animals. In nature they eat whatever they can find, frequently nibbling on mushrooms, leaves, rotting fruit or vegetables, small insects, or dead animals. Those raising crickets for human consumption and resale typically choose a commercial cricket feed, often one that is certified organic.

While cricket farms vary in size and specifics, the general production process is the same whether you're trying to raise 1,000 or 10 million crickets. When it comes time for breeding, cricket farmers place pans filled with soil for the insects into their bins. The crickets lay their eggs—which look like miniature grains of rice—in the soil. Each female typically lays between 100 and 200 eggs. Once the eggs are produced, the pans are moved to their own bins for hatching.

It only takes about a week for cricket eggs to hatch. As crickets grow, they live in bins that have been customized with cut-outs covered with landscape fabric or fine wire screen that allows for ventilation but keeps tiny crickets from escaping. Bins are filled with loosely stacked cardboard egg cartons that create nooks and crannies where crickets can hide. Crickets like their own territory and they prefer small, dark spaces.

After the crickets mature and lay eggs—about seven weeks after they hatch—they can be harvested. Cricket slaughter is considerably less bloody than traditional butchering. In fact, there's zero bloodshed when crickets are harvested. Insects are simply transferred into resealable plastic bags and placed in a freezer, where they go into a state of hibernation before dying.

The US Food and Drug Administration doesn't have specific guidelines that regulate edible insect farming or production. The agency is relying on laws set forth in the Food, Drug, and Cosmetic Act to govern the industry. Key guidelines include:

* Bugs and insects are considered food if intended for eating.
* Insects must be raised specifically for human consumption following current good manufacturing practices.

* Insects raised for animal or pet food use cannot be sold as human food.
* Food must be clean and wholesome and produced, packaged, stored, and transported under sanitary conditions.
* Insects sold as food cannot be collected in the wild owing to the risk of carrying disease or pesticides.

Beyond just plain crickets, many farmers are selling roasted insects flavored with everything from spicy cayenne to dill pickle and cinnamon to pumpkin spice. Others are grinding harvested crickets into protein powder. They're selling the powder and products made with it, such as flour, protein bars, cookies, brownie mix, and chips.

Because production costs are so high and demand exceeds supply, cricket farmers can command a high price for their products. In early 2021, for example, a pound of ground cricket powder retailed for around $50, and a snack pack–sized bag containing approximately 75 whole roasted crickets sold for $3. Industry insiders predict that prices will come down significantly by 2025 as processes are automated and farmers are able to produce larger batches of crickets.

Beyond edible items, many cricket producers are also selling cricket "frass" as fertilizer. Frass is a mixture of cricket poop and exoskeletons that crickets shed as they grow. Chitin is a naturally occurring substance found in those exoskeletons and it's believed to help jumpstart a plant's immune system. Crickets produce a lot of frass. In fact, most farmers find they can harvest frass equal to half their cricket production by weight. For example, if a farm produces 500 pounds (227 kg) of crickets per month, about 250 pounds (113 kg) of frass also is being produced. The added revenue from selling that poo can make a real difference—cricket frass retails for upward of $10 per pound.

Researchers at England's University of Leeds say chitin has potential that far exceeds fertilizer. If chitin could be efficiently extracted from insect exoskeletons, they say it could be used to preserve food. It can also be used to make surgical thread or glue.

Potential is what most insect farmers in the Western world are counting on for now. They believe the crickets they're raising could become exactly the type of protein needed to feed the world's growing population.

Frass can give plants' immune systems a boost.

4

Powered by Bugs

Tammy Mann was spending hours each week swimming, biking, and running as part of her triathlon training when she first learned about cricket protein. "I was training with a group and everyone was talking about how they were training and what they were eating," says Mann. "I have a lot of gut health issues and I'm gluten intolerant, so it definitely caught my attention when someone mentioned cricket powder."[5]

Mann went home, fired up her computer, and did some research. She found a company in the United Kingdom selling cricket protein powder, so she ordered some.

"As soon as I got it, I used it to make a smoothie," she says. "It was gritty and, frankly, I was kind of grossed out. But it was expensive and I wanted to give it a try, so I used it every day until the container was empty." Mann didn't change anything else about her diet or training, but said she quickly began to notice changes.

"My body became leaner, I was stronger and more energized," she says. "I usually got hungry an hour into my workout, but the cricket powder smoothies really sustained me. There were so many positives, I just kept thinking, 'It's too bad it tastes so bad.'"

Mann wasn't keen on the idea of ordering another expensive container of foul-tasting cricket powder, but she was intrigued. She started researching. She read articles about insect nutrition, the global food crisis, and the impact food production has on the environment.

"That's when I decided not to give up," Mann says. She started ordering cricket powder from as many different places as she could find. She made her daily smoothie, switching out only the cricket powder. After trying about ten brands, Mann began to realize all cricket protein was not created equal: Taste varied depending upon the species of cricket, what they'd been fed, and how they'd been harvested. That revelation inspired more experimentation. She started making protein bars, which she shared with friends and family. Soon, she branched into cookie baking. In early 2020, she quit her longtime job as a designer and founded her own cricket cookie and protein bar business called Harmony Cricket Farm. Based in the western Minneapolis suburb of Golden Valley, Mann is now selling her own products online and through retail outlets.

"I'm not one to force these things on anybody," she says. "But I'm finding there are a lot of people who are mindful about the environment and sustainability who want to incorporate insects into their diets. Plus, there are athletes and people who simply want to eat a little healthier. The nutrition is very appealing to a lot of people."

Sure, nutrition matters to triathletes, professional football players, and adults who suddenly find they no longer fit into their pants. But do kids really need to focus on vitamins and minerals?

"Good nutrition is important to young people because it's what helps your body stay healthy and strong," says registered dietitian Lisa Lovejoy. "Eating food that's good for you helps you grow. Healthy eating gives you energy and keeps you focused so you can do things like ride your bike, dance, play soccer, or do well in school."[6]

The topic of nutrition was front and center when the Food and Agriculture Organization of the United Nations issued its 200-

page report suggesting that eating insects could both address the current problem of world hunger and the future challenge of feeding a growing population.

The nutritional value of insects varies based on the type of insect, the insect's diet, and the way in which the insect was processed or prepared. Caterpillars, for instance, contain about three times the fat content of grasshoppers. The stage of life an insect is at when it's harvested—egg, larva, adult—also affects its nutritional makeup. There is still a lot of research to be done on the specifics of insect nutrition, and later consumer education. But early studies reveal that insects such as crickets, palm weevil larvae, and mealworms are as healthy—if not healthier—as beef or chicken. Overall, edible insects are regarded as an excellent source of protein, minerals, and fats.

PROTEIN

When people talk about insect nutrition, they often shine the spotlight on protein. Protein helps build strong bones, muscles, tendons, cartilage, skin, and blood. Your hair, fingernails, and toenails are mostly comprised of a type of protein called keratin. The human body cannot store protein, so it's something you need to eat every day.

Among the most popular edible insects, mealworms pack the biggest protein punch. Pound for pound, mealworms contain nearly twice as much protein as lean chicken breast.

How do other insects stack up? Grasshoppers contain 20 grams of protein in a 100-gram serving. Crickets contain 12.9 grams of protein. That's comparable to the 14 grams of protein in a 100 gram-serving of lean ground beef.

IRON

Your body needs iron to produce blood. Iron helps move oxygen from your lungs to your tissues and helps regulate your body temperature. People who don't get enough iron often feel tired and have trouble focusing.

Beef is considered a good source of iron. A 3.5-ounce (100 grams) serving of lean steak contains 3.66 milligrams of iron. A 3.5-ounce serving of crickets provides more than three times as much iron—12.91 milligrams. Other insects rich in iron include mopane worms (31 mg iron/100 g), mealworms (7.0 mg/100 g), buffalo worms (6.8 mg/100 g), and red ants (6 mg/100 g).

OTHER VITAMINS AND MINERALS

Vitamin B12 helps keep the body's nerves and blood cells healthy. It also helps make DNA, the genetic material in all cells.

Salmon has long been considered a good source of Vitamin B12, with about 3 micrograms per 100-gram (3.5 oz) serving. Depending upon what they're fed and whether they're harvested as adults or nymphs, crickets contain two to three times more Vitamin B12 than salmon. Crickets weigh in at 5.4 to 8.7 micrograms per 100 gram serving.

Mopane worms and palm weevil larvae are good sources of zinc, which your body needs to fight off bacteria and viruses. Grasshoppers, locusts, beetles, and crickets are rich in folic acid, which helps your body produce and maintain new cells.

FIBER

There are two types of fiber—soluble and insoluble. Both are important for health, digestion, and preventing disease.

Most insects' bodies are made of chitin, which is an insoluble fiber. It passes through the body, moving food through your digestive system, and scrubbing bacteria out of your intestines. In addition to helping with digestion, researchers say it supports the growth of good bacteria in your gut.

A recent study conducted at the University of Wisconsin-Madison found that eating just 25 grams of cricket powder per day can positively affect your digestive health. That amounts to less than three tablespoons of cricket powder each day, blended into smoothies or baked into muffins.

Of course, just tossing some cricket powder into brownie batter or cookie dough won't magically transform them into health food. Cricket powder will ensure there's a little more protein or iron than there would have been without it, but it cannot completely offset the fat or sugar in those treats.

There is still much to learn about the nutrition and digestibility of different insects. There are also debates over whether insects can fit into certain restrictive diets. Vegetarians don't eat animals. Vegans do not eat or use animal products. Technically, insects are animals. They are members of the phylum Arthropoda, which also includes arachnids (spiders, scorpions), centipedes (centipedes, millipedes) and crustaceans (crabs, lobsters, crayfish, shrimp). So, the simple answer is no. Vegetarians and vegans do not eat insects. Except, when it comes to humans, nothing is simple.

People adopt vegetarian or vegan diets for a variety of reasons. Family preferences, concerns about animal rights or the environment, and health issues are some of the most common reasons for choosing vegetarianism or veganism. If you shoo away mosquitoes instead of swatting them and get teary at the sight of a dead squirrel along the side of the road, you probably won't be willing to add insects to your diet. But if the environment and health are your main concerns, insects may well find a place on your dinner plate.

Josh Galt is a vegan who eats insects. He calls himself an "entovegan." It is a term and movement he introduced when he spoke at the North American Coalition for Insect Agriculture's 2018 Eating Insects Athens conference in Georgia. "People in the industry always talk about insect protein, protein, protein," Galt said. "The thing is, you can get all the protein you need from plants, you really can. Gut health and Vitamin B12, and minerals—now, those are selling points. Especially the Vitamin B12. That's a gap in the vegan diet that can't be filled by eating plants."[7] Animal products are the main source of Vitamin B12, so plant-based eaters are often forced to turn to supplements to ensure their dietary needs are being met.

Today, Galt advises insect-based companies trying to market their products to vegans, and he counsels vegans who are considering adding edible insects to their diets. His entovegan movement has drawn harsh criticism from by-the-book vegans who say he is simply trying to cash in on veganism's growing popularity. At the same time, he has inspired some vegetarians—now called entovegetarians—to create their own insect-inclusive diets.

Veganism, vegetarianism, entoveganism, and entovegetarianism are all lifestyle choices. But some diets are driven by religious beliefs. Many of those beliefs are based on books or guidelines written thousands of years ago. Scholars who study them often disagree about what the writings specifically allow when it comes to eating insects.

Locusts, for example, were eaten at the time of Mohammed and are considered a halal or lawful food in Islam, according to the Salafi Centre in Manchester, England. Other scholars of Islam have debated permissible locust species and methods of killing. The Torah prohibits eating worms and insects, except for locusts. Jewish scholars, for the most part, agree that four types of desert locust—red, yellow, spotted gray, and white—can be considered kosher. The first of Buddhism's Five Precepts is to avoid harming any living thing, so entomophagy is a no-go for many who practice that religion. But the Dalai Lama and many other Tibetan Buddhists do eat meat in certain circumstances.

Obviously, entomophagy is relatively new in Western culture. That means there's still much to be learned, discussed, and debated. Most nutritional data collected at this point, for instance, focuses on a limited number of insect species and little of it addresses spoilage or contamination. As the practice of eating insects becomes more widespread, more money can be invested in research. More attention from medical, nutritional, and agricultural experts could lead to new revelations about the ways in which bugs may help nourish the world.

5

Burping, Farting Cows

It's only natural to giggle at the mention of cow burps and farts. You imagine a whole field of Holstein or Angus cattle, peacefully grazing in a grassy meadow and then—*BWAAAAAP!*

Burping and farting are natural. You, your aunt Shirley, your teacher—everybody does it. Farting is also common in the animal kingdom. Mammals and some reptiles fart. (Scientists aren't sure about amphibians; there's some debate about whether their sphincter muscles are strong enough to create the pressure necessary for farting.)

What is certain is that flatulence—the medical term for farting, passing wind, or having gas—is mainly the result of digestion. The microbes in our guts work to break down food. As they work, those microbes produce gases like carbon dioxide and methane; some of those gases are released as flatulence.

Eructation is a fancy word for burping or belching. In humans, it is the body's way of expelling excess air from the upper digestive tract. Swallowing excess air is the cause of most burping. That air never reaches the stomach and, instead, accumulates in the esophagus until it's released through your mouth.

METHANE

Cows are ruminant animals; other ruminants include sheep, goats, buffalo, elk, deer, giraffes, and camels. These animals have digestive systems that are very different from those of humans. Instead of one stomach compartment, they have four. The rumen is the first and largest compartment. It is filled with billions of microbes that begin to break down the grass and hay that ruminants eat. As those foods break down, the microbes create methane and carbon dioxide. When cows belch, they release these gases into the atmosphere (far more than they release by farting).

Methane and carbon dioxide are significant contributors to climate change.

Certain gases let heat pass through the atmosphere, but they prevent it from leaving. These gases are called greenhouse gases. Methane and carbon dioxide are both greenhouse gases, but methane grabs more headlines because it is 28 times more powerful at trapping heat in the atmosphere than carbon dioxide. The trapped heat is causing the Earth to get warmer; this is called global warming.

One warm day is nothing to fret about. But the Earth's air temperatures have been rising for a long time. Overall, temperatures now are about two degrees Fahrenheit (16.67°C) hotter than they were 150 years ago. These warmer temperatures have resulted in rising sea levels, melting glaciers, stronger storms, hotter summers, longer lasting droughts, and more frequent wildfires. These long-term changes are called climate change.

Coal-burning power plants, oil-drilling sites, gas-guzzling cars, wetlands, and livestock production all produce greenhouse gases that contribute to global warming. Livestock—thanks to eructation, flatulence, and manure storage—is responsible for about 14.5 percent of the world's greenhouse gas emissions. But pigs, chickens, and sheep aren't even in the same league as cattle when it comes to producing greenhouse gases. Cattle—raised both for beef and milk—are responsible for approximately 65 percent of all greenhouse gas emissions created by livestock. A single cow is thought to produce between 154 and 340 pounds (70 to 154 kg) of methane each year. Worldwide, there are about 1.5 billion cattle producing a whopping 231 billion to 510 billion pounds (105 billion to 231 billion kg) of methane per year.

No doubt about it, people love hamburgers, steaks, cheese, and ice cream. But 510 billion pounds (231 billion kg) of methane is a lot, and consumers are becoming increasingly aware of sustainability and doing what's right for the environment. This has led scientists to try to come up with ways to reduce emissions from cattle. They've tried breeding animals that burp less and planting trees that will help remove carbon dioxide from the air. Researchers also are experimenting with adding seaweed, fats, and oils to cows' diets, all in an effort to reduce methane production.

So, why all this talk about gassy cows in a book about eating insects? Insects and bugs also produce methane, but significantly less than traditional livestock.

Does that mean bugs fart? Probably. There's no definitive scientific answer about how insects release digestive gases. North Carolina State University assistant professor of entomology Aram Mikaelyan, for one, thinks it's likely some of that gas is released via the anus. He's done extensive research into bacteria growth in the guts of termites. "I doubt insects fart in the traditional sense. I don't think it's a burst of gas. It's unlikely their sphincters would be strong enough to allow gas to build up," Mikaelyan says. "Most of the methane an insect produces is made in its hindgut, which is close to the anus. So, some gas probably comes out when they poop, plus there's a good chance there's additional seepage."[8]

Could you smell a bug fart? Unlikely, says Mikaelyan, "If they have diets high in protein, that ends up as sulphur, which could be smelly. But remember, we're talking about teeny, tiny, miniscule bits of gas."

And what about bug belching? Some research indicates that gases produced through digestion are released through a bug's spiracles. Spiracles are respiratory openings found on the thorax or abdomen of an insect. Mikaelyan notes, "Because of their anatomy and digestive processes, we don't think insects belch in the same sense humans or cows or goats do."

There are a few types of bugs that are big greenhouse gas producers. Cockroaches, termites, centipedes, and various arthropods all produce methane when digesting food, in a similar way to cattle. In fact, some researchers believe termites alone are responsible for 1 percent to 3 percent of the world's methane emissions, though the structure of their mounds effectively filters out and breaks down half those emissions before they are released into the atmosphere. The good news is that cockroaches, termites, and centipedes are not exactly popular menu items, so there aren't massive farms pumping tons of cockroach emissions into the atmosphere.

According to the Food and Agriculture Organization of the United Nations, mealworm larvae, crickets, and locusts—all deemed viable for human consumption in the Western world—are thought to release 80 to 100 times less methane than cattle.

Want to talk about carbon dioxide? For every 220 pounds (100 kg) of pork produced, more than 6 pounds (2.7 kg) of carbon dioxide is released into the atmosphere. For 220 pounds of beef produced, 79 pounds (36 kg) of carbon dioxide is released. By comparison, the same 220 pounds of crickets (which is a whole lot of crickets), emits 0.002 pounds (907 mg) of carbon dioxide, less than the weight of a single raisin.

WATER

Lower greenhouse gas emissions are just one way in which eating insects is more environmentally friendly than munching on bacon cheeseburgers. Water is another huge consideration.

More than 785 million people around the world lack everyday access to clean water. For 2.7 billion people, water is scarce at least one month per year. In developing countries, women walk an average of 3.5 miles (5.6 km) per day to gather water for their families.

If you think water scarcity is a problem only for people in faraway places, you are sadly mistaken. Nearly the entire state of California suffered through drought conditions from December 2011 to March 2019, a period during which the state's governor ordered cities to reduce water use by 25 percent. California residents were told not to water their lawns or wash their cars. The state's dry land led to increasingly dusty air and local hospitals reported an increase in patients suffering from breathing problems.

How is this possible? Isn't 70 percent of the world covered by water? Well, yes, it is, but only 2.5 percent of that is fresh, unpolluted, and safe to drink.

Researchers with the US Forest Service predict that, by 2071, nearly half the 204 freshwater basins in the United States may not be able to meet the country's monthly water demand. There are a couple of reasons for this. First, the United States will simply have more people. In addition, thanks to higher temperatures and less rain and snow, the water supply itself will decrease.

Right about now you're probably thinking, *Well, I don't use that much water.* And, chances are, you are wrong. The average American directly uses about 88 gallons (333 l) of water each day. Your five-minute shower takes 20 gallons (76 l) of water. You use about 5 gallons (19 l) of water if you leave the water running while brushing your teeth. You flush away 1.6 gallons (6 l) of water every time you, well, flush. And indirectly, you're using way, way more water. Indirect water use refers to the water that is used to produce things, such as food, books, furniture, and clothing. The majority of the world's water is used for agriculture, industry, and electricity.

Remember, plants need water to grow. Cattle, hogs, and chickens need water to drink. Water is also necessary to grow the feed those animals eat. In the United States, it takes about 1,300 gallons (4,921 l) of water to produce each person's food. That's not per week; it takes that much water every single day. How is that possible? Well, it adds up quickly. Consider this:

* It takes more than 100 gallons (379 l) of water just to produce your breakfast. A glass of orange juice alone takes 45 gallons (170 l). That includes the water needed to process the juice and irrigate the orchard. Orange trees are thirsty things. A single navel orange tree, for example, needs an average 15.6 gallons (59 l) of water every day. It can take three or more years before the tree produces any fruit and then, when it begins producing oranges, the fruit takes 7 to 8 months to ripen. And that glass of juice is just the beginning. It will take another 50 gallons (189 l) to produce your morning egg, and 11 gallons (42 l) for a slice of toast.

* A single slice of sausage pizza for lunch takes approximately 170 gallons (644 l) of water to produce: 18 (68 l) for the flour, 21 (79 l) for the cheese, 2.5 (9 l) for the sauce, and 129 (488 l) for the sausage. Add 48 gallons (182 l) for the glass of milk at the end.

* Hungry for an afterschool candy bar? That takes another 450 gallons (1,703 l). Cocoa plants are thirsty little things.

* An evening cookout will take another 891 gallons (3,373 l) of water to produce: 626 gallons (2,370 l) for a cheeseburger and 265 gallons (1,003 l) for a serving of baked beans.

Short of giving up showers and food, is there a way to live a life that runs on less water?

Yes, there is. Traditional farming is water intensive. Globally, producing crops such as wheat and corn, and raising livestock including beef, hogs, and chickens, accounts for 92 percent of our water footprint. The term "water footprint" is used to describe the amount of fresh water that a process or activity uses. In the United States, the meat we eat accounts for about one-third of our water footprint. Let's focus on beef cattle for a minute. It takes about 18 months for a cow to be ready to go to market. During those 18 months, the animal drinks water and eats grains and grasses that have been irrigated. Water is also needed for processing. In the end, it takes about 1,800 gallons (6,814 l) of water to produce a pound of beef. And cows aren't the only big water users. It takes 576 gallons (2,180 l) of water to produce a pound of pork, and 500 gallons (1,893 l) to produce a pound of chicken.

But it takes only one gallon (3.8 l) of water to produce a pound (.45 kg) of crickets. A pound of mealworms can be produced with just a half gallon (1.9 l) of water.

Launching yourself into an insect-only diet probably isn't going to happen. But what if you substituted bugs for meat just one day per week?

If a typical family of four got their protein one day per week from insects, in one year they would save approximately 172,000 gallons (651,000 l) of water. That's a lot of water. Now imagine if every family in the United States did the same thing. That would be a savings of about 14 trillion gallons (53 trillion l) of water each year. Another 860 billion gallons (3.3 trillion l) of water could be saved if all the families in Canada joined in on the idea of eating bugs one day per week.

It may sound crazy, but most big movements start small. Have you ever heard of Meatless Mondays? It's a campaign that started in 2003, encouraging people to skip eating meat just one day per week. Meatless Mondays started in the United States and has grown into a global effort. It is officially recognized in countries including Argentina, Australia, Belgium, Croatia, and Israel.

Can eating insects single-handedly save the world? Probably not. But it would make a difference. People in Western countries are realizing that finding more environmentally friendly and sustainable protein sources must be a priority. Scientists are experimenting with other alternatives, such as meat grown in laboratories, seaweed, duckweed, and micro-algae. Edible insects could very well be the environmental difference-maker we've all been looking for.

6

What's Slowing the Bug Trend?

What will it take for people to change their mind-sets from "Oh, no, ants are ruining our picnic," to "Oh, yum, we're eating ants at our picnic"?

Ask six different people what would prevent them from eating insects and you'll likely get six different answers. Too strange. Too gross. Too new. Too unknown. Too hard to find. Too expensive.

Charles Wilson thinks it is probably a combination of many of these things. Wilson, founder and chief operating officer of a company in Portland, Oregon, called Cricket Flours, says his reasons for getting into the industry were personal. "Growing up, our family always had dietary restrictions due to food allergies," he says.[9] In 2013, he started experimenting with alternative flours and proteins. Charles came across articles promoting the use of edible insects as a sustainable source of protein. He started blending cricket protein smoothies and fine-tuning recipes. In 2014, he started his company, where growth has been slow but steady.

"For a lot of people, it comes down to opportunity. I had to do research to learn that cricket protein was a viable option," says

Wilson. "How can people try cricket protein if they don't even know it exists? Once they try it and like it, we often hear, 'Oh, I'd have used this sooner if I'd known about it,' or 'I'd use this more if it wasn't so expensive.'"

Cost is undeniably a factor. One pound (.45 kg) of 100 percent cricket powder sells for $40 to $50. A tiny half-ounce jar (about 14 g) of culinary-grade black ants costs approximately $30. One cup (about 200 g) of black soldier fly larvae will set you back about $36. Compare these costs to a pound of lean ground beef at about $6 per pound or organic chicken breasts at $8 per pound. Even alternative proteins, such as 100 percent pure soy powder ($16 per pound), 100 percent hemp seed powder ($17 per pound), and 100 percent pure pea powder ($10 per pound), currently are more affordable.

What is it about insect protein that makes it so expensive? A lot of the price has to do with scale. That is a fancy way of saying small farms, whether they're raising chickens or cows or crickets, are less efficient than large ones. And that means the food grown on those small farms is going to cost more than food grown on large farms.

Worldwide, insect farming is still very much a manual operation. Shelby Smith, founder of Gym-N-Eat Crickets in central Iowa, often works 100 hours per week, feeding and watering, checking temperatures, changing out pie pans of dirt, cleaning bins, harvesting and roasting crickets, monitoring temperatures. She's also the chief recipe developer, protein bar baker, marketer, as well as director of packaging, sales, and distribution. She sets up booths at several farmers' markets each week, manages her website and social media accounts, has meetings to try to get her products into stores, delivers products to supermarkets, and speaks to dozens of schools and community organizations each month. For small farms and the farmers who run them, there are no shortcuts. There are no days off.

A few large-scale, automated operations to produce crickets, mealworms, black soldier fly larvae, and waxworms have begun popping up in North America and Europe. As farms get larger, it makes sense to buy feed and other supplies in bulk. It's easier to justify investing in labor-saving machinery and technology, or in the employees needed to design those machines and technology. Large-scale production requires research in everything from insect biology and optimal diets, to taste testing, consumer response, and to advertising. Yes, there are larger start-up costs, but eventually they result in savings. Those savings mean the cost per unit—in this case, a pound of crickets—goes down. Until then, insect products remain a high-priced protein option.

Beyond cost, there are still a whole lot of people out there who simply have no idea the entomophagy movement exists. And even if they do know about it, they don't know about the nutrition or sustainability aspects, so they don't understand why it should matter to them.

In the United States farmers participate in something called "checkoff programs." When farmers sell their products, they are required to pay a certain percentage of their income into a national fund related to that specific product. For example, the beef checkoff program collects one dollar for every cow sold. There are checkoff programs for producers of specific agricultural products such as soybeans, milk, mushrooms, almonds, and potatoes. Those funds are used to conduct research, develop new products, and advertise that specific commodity. These checkoff funds have helped pay for marketing campaigns developed by some of the world's top advertising firms. Chances are you've heard some of these slogans: "Got Milk," "Pork. The Other White Meat," "The Incredible Edible Egg," or "Beef: It's What's for Dinner."

The beef checkoff alone typically brings in more than $40 million per year. That cash allows industry organizations such as the National Cattlemen's Beef Association to hire famous actors to pitch their products. If you watch TV or listen to the radio, chances are you've heard Academy Award–winning actor Matthew McConaughey urge you to eat a steak.

And it's not just the beef industry itself that has folks craving red meat. McDonald's, the largest single purchaser of beef in the world, sells somewhere around 50 million burgers every single day. In 2019, the company spent $447.3 million on advertising world-wide, whetting consumers' appetites for Quarter Pounders and fur-ther fueling the public's ongoing love of all things beef.

It's not that insect industry insiders don't want to advertise. They would love to. But they don't have the cash for a beef- or pork-sized marketing blitz. There are no insect checkoff dollars. There are no paid celebrity spokespeople. There are no McDonald's-sized mealworm vendors, no coordinated digital media campaigns, and no iconic catch phrases. In fact, the North American Coalition for Insect Agriculture (NACIA) only got its start in 2016. The group's membership fees range from free for K–12 students to $500 for corporate memberships. In late 2020, the NACIA had fewer than 75 members from all of North America. Those membership fees—plus a handful of donations—make up its entire budget. The orga-nization is dedicated to education and awareness, but it's unlikely you'll see a commercial for roasted ants airing on national TV any-time soon.

"We simply don't have the money," says Cheryl Preyer, NACIA president. "We're doing simple things, like a quarterly newsletter for members and an annual meeting, a portion of which is open to the public. We are basically a volunteer organization. We have a lot of passion, but we don't yet have many resources."[10]

Which brings us back to the challenge that people will not buy what they don't know about. It's common sense, but it's also backed by research. A 2018 study conducted in Finland, Sweden, Germany, and the Czech Republic found that consumers who had been educated about the sustainability and nutrition of insect-based foods were willing try them and pay more for them. Education, marketing, and an effort to develop products that look appealing and taste good has made a difference in countries such as Belgium and the Netherlands.

At this point, it's not terribly difficult to find whole roasted crickets, mealworms, or black ants. They may not be prominently displayed on the shelves of your local grocery store, but they can often be purchased at farmers' markets or through online shops. But let's be blunt: most people find it easier to eat insects if they don't look like insects. Insect powder is incredibly versatile and can be used to add protein to anything from pizza dough to brownies. If you go on the hunt for prepackaged items made with insect powder, you will find a few companies making cookies, cricket chips, and a whole lot of cricket protein bars. However, the product selection is extremely limited. That's because these small insect producers, who are doing it all themselves, can't afford to make more than a product or two.

It's probably going to take a major food company, like Nestlé, General Mills, or Kraft Heinz, to start adding insect protein to some of their products before we begin to see broad availability of a large number of insect-based foods. These huge corporations have the research, development, and marketing teams necessary to launch new, appealing products. Perhaps you will someday be able to buy Cheerios fortified with mealworm protein, Stouffer's lasagna made with cricket powder, or even Kraft Maca-wormy & Cheese.

Many say more research needs to be done before major corporations—and billions of consumers—are willing to take a chance on entomophagy. Scientists meeting in Sweden in early 2019 cautioned against mass production of insects as food until more studies can be conducted regarding insects' housing and feed requirements, waste management, and putting systems in place to ensure that escaping insects don't damage the ecosystem.

Further research must be done on possible allergies and toxins that could be associated with edible insects. Safety procedures are essential but, at this point, barely exist. The US government, for example, has rules about how many insect parts can show up in a can of pears before it's considered inedible, but there aren't many guidelines for the production of edible insects.

Another challenge? Entomophobia. This very real disorder is defined as "an abnormal and persistent fear of insects." Sufferers experience anxiety even though they realize that most insects pose no threat. In *The Infested Mind: Why Humans, Fear, Loathe, and Love Insects*, author Jeffrey Lockwood estimates about 6 percent of those living in the United States suffer from some form of entomophobia. Six percent may not seem like much, but it represents nearly 20 million people.

Chapman University, located in Orange, California, regularly conducts a survey on American fears. In 2016, researchers indicated that 25 percent of those questioned said they were afraid of insects and/or spiders. That's more than feared heights, a devastating natural disaster, or being mugged.

Could you eat something you feared? Possibly, but the answer to this question varies by individual. How severe is the fear? Do they know why they fear bugs? Does it have to do with a fear of germs or disease? Do they have a desire to overcome their fear? Is it possible they're fearful of living insects but are fine consuming insect powder? In general, if those fearful of insects have the option to eat other things, it seems pretty unlikely they'll choose to dine on bugs.

Let's also acknowledge that there are many people who aren't fearful of insects, but who are disgusted by the thought of eating them. That's a notion that's explored at the Disgusting Food Museum. Located in Malmo, Sweden, and with pop-up exhibits that have traveled around the globe, the museum acknowledges that disgust is one of the six fundamental human emotions. "While the emotion is universal, the foods that we find disgusting are not," reads the description on the museum's website. "What is delicious to one person can be revolting to another."[11]

The museum includes a tasting bar where a dozen or more disgusting foods are available for sampling. Westerners often cringe when a live octopus is cut into small pieces and served while it's still moving. Known as *san-nakji*, the dish is a delicacy in Korea.

Haggis, made of ground animal organs mixed with oatmeal and boiled in a bag made from a sheep's stomach, might not be your cup of tea, but the savory pudding is the national dish of Scotland. Entomophagy is represented at the museum by crunchy locusts, a popular snack food in Israel, and a maggot-infested sheep's milk cheese called *casu marzu* from the Italian island of Sardinia.

And, yes, there are foods regularly consumed by Americans that made their way into the museum's Display of Disgust: root beer, Spam, Twinkies, and Pop-Tarts. If you find yourself defending the sweet deliciousness of a freshly toasted Pop-Tart, remember that someone in Scotland is probably muttering the same thing about their scrumptious haggis. What is a comfort food to you is not a comfort food to everyone everywhere. That is the message the museum is hoping to get across. Curator Samuel West wants visitors to challenge their notions about what is and isn't edible. "Our aim is to open people's minds" says West.[12]

NACIA's Cheryl Preyer has high hopes that young people, with access to a wider variety of culinary options than their parents or grandparents, might open their minds and be more willing to try new things—even haggis, maggot cheese, and especially insects. "For most people, if they haven't eaten a bug by the time they're 40 years old, they're probably thinking, 'Why would I start now?' It's all about familiarity," she says. "But Millennials, and Gen Z'ers, and beyond . . . they've all been exposed to a broader food palate than most of us were at their ages. They have the Internet and YouTube and a hundred other ways to learn about the world around them. I think that may spark an openness."[13]

It is unlikely insects will be featured in Happy Meals or on school lunch menus anytime soon. Change takes time. But a combination of education, marketing, and lowered costs may eventually convince diners to add insect protein to their diet—at least once in a while.

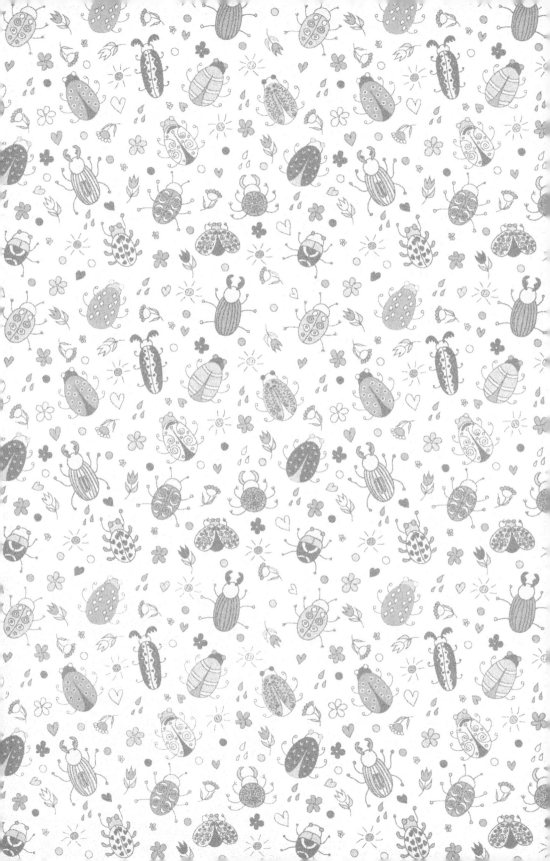

7

I Swallowed a What?

Before we get started here, it is important that you not freak out. No matter what, you're going to remain calm and reasonable.

Great. So, there's something you should know: even if you don't intentionally eat insects, you are eating insects. It's true! In fact, there's a good chance you had some this morning, or at least within the past few days. That's because there are insect wings, legs, and eggs in many of the foods you eat daily. Most of those bug bits aren't there on purpose. They are in your vegetables and juice and snacks because those foods are grown on farms, processed in plants, and transported in trucks where bugs sometimes happen to be.

The US Food and Drug Administration (FDA) has guidelines that allow for a certain percentage of "natural contaminants" in our food. Those contaminants include, among other things, mold, rot, rodent hairs, maggots, and, yes, insects. The agency publishes and regularly updates a guide called *Food Defect Levels Handbook*. In it, the FDA lists acceptable levels of "defects" for more than 100 foods and beverages, ranging from apricots to tomato soup.

Skim through the list and you will learn that a teaspoon of ground allspice can contain an average of 30 or more insect fragments. The FDA allows an average of 60 or more of these teeny bugs in every cup of frozen broccoli. A can of peaches can contain an average of one small larva. The FDA lists "average" defect counts because there's no way testing can be done on every single bag or can. Instead, samples are taken and as long as the average number of offenses is within range, the products are considered edible.

Before you decide to cut allspice, frozen veggies, and canned fruits out of your diet, understand that some of your favorite foods may also have "defects." A small glass of orange juice, for example, can contain five or more fly eggs. A slice of bread with two table-spoons of peanut butter can contain 64 insect fragments. One cup of macaroni and cheese can include 100 insect parts. The wheat flour, tomato sauce, and oregano that goes into pizza means you could be eating as many as 90 insect fragments or fly eggs per slice. And that yummy chocolate bar you just devoured? It could contain 30 or more insect parts.

When the researchers at the FDA meet to review and update defect standards, they consider whether the foreign matter in our food is "offensive to the senses." That means they're not so worried about bug wings and rodent hairs being dangerous, they simply want to keep the ick factor low. You won't fuss over what you can't see, taste, or smell.

If you stop to think about the ways in which foods are harvested, it's easy to imagine how those defects get into foods. Wheat, for example, grows on farms. Those fields are not sterile bubbles. Rather, they're filled with soil, weeds, insects, birds, and rodents. Huge, drivable machines called combines are used to harvest the wheat. These machines "combine" the tasks of cutting the wheat and shaking the grains away from their stalks. When a combine fills, it is emptied into large wagons or trucks, which are taken to storage bins on the farm or straight to the mill. Flour mills have machines that sort sticks, weeds, and stones out of the grain, but bug parts are often so small they simply cannot be sifted out.

The FDA says its defect limits "have been established because it is economically impractical to grow, harvest, or process raw products that are totally free of non-hazardous, naturally occurring, unavoidable defects."[14]

"Farms and processing plants are clean, but they're not as sterile as, let's say, an operating room," says Los Angeles–based food safety expert Jeff Nelken. "There are things, like high levels of mercury in seafood or herbicides in vegetables that are definitely harmful for people to consume. But these microscopic bug parts have been determined to be safe—at least at certain levels."[15]

A handful of researchers, consumer advocates, and journalists have tried to use these FDA guidelines to determine how many flies, maggots, and mites the average person unintentionally eats each year. Their calculations vary widely, from a measly four ounces (97 g) to as much as two pounds (0.9 kg). Even if you fall at the low end of that range, it's likely you are inadvertently eating at least a half million infect fragments each year.

Beyond these "defects," there are times when manufacturers are intentionally adding insect parts or powder to your food. Carmine is a natural red dye made from the cochineal scale, an insect scientifically known as *Dactylopius coccus*. Lots of people call these bugs "beetles," but they're not—they're scales. Scale insects thrive in warm, dry environments. They are oval, about the size of a BB, often with no visible legs or antennae. Cochineals live on the prickly pear cactus. They are white or light gray—until they're squished. That's when their plump bellies burst with dark red liquid. That scarlet liquid is the cochineal scale's weapon against its number one predator: the ant.

The cochineal scale is native to Mexico and South America. The bugs are primarily farmed in Peru, where they are sun-dried and crushed to create a red pigment used to color textiles, cosmetics, and food. Many manufacturers add the color to products to make them more appealing and more appetizing. Different companies identify the pigment by different names, but if you see cochineal, carmine, carminic acid, crimson lake, natural red 4, or E120 on a food label, you know at least part of its coloring came from insects.

The use of this natural dye dates back at least five centuries and, until recently, was widely used by major companies. In 2012, Starbucks came under attack for using carmine to color items ranging from its Strawberry Crème Frappuccino and Strawberry Banana Smoothie to its Raspberry Swirl Pound Cake and Red Velvet Whoopie Pie. Some customers, including many vegetarians and vegans, were outraged. The media caught wind of the controversy and headlines like "Starbucks Puts Dead Beetles in Frappuccinos" and "Is That a Crushed Bug in Your Frothy Starbucks Drink?" started appearing in media around the world.

Starbucks initially defended its use of carmine as a "natural product." Later, the company decided to ditch carmine, saying, "While it is a safe product that poses no health risk, we are reviewing alternative natural ingredients."[16]

While generally safe, cochineal extract has been shown to pose health risks to some people by triggering allergies and asthma. In 2009, the FDA started requiring that foods and cosmetics containing cochineal extract list it on their labels.

Starbucks' red foods and drinks now get their color from lycopene, a natural, tomato-based extract. Other companies have switched to natural food coloring alternatives made from berries, beets, or potatoes. But that doesn't mean cochineal-colored foods can't be found in your pantry or refrigerator. Hershey's Good & Plenty candy, Nature Made's gummy vitamins, Mentos' Rainbow Roll, Tropicana's Ruby Red Grapefruit juice drink, Werther's Original Sugar-Free Caramel Cinnamon Hard Candies, Willa Wonka's Nerds and Gobstoppers, and Yoplait's strawberry yogurt are just a few of the food products that still get their coloring from the cochineal scale.

Sometimes what you're eating doesn't contain bugs or insects, but rather the secretions of those creatures. Honey is a widely loved sweetener. But let's not kid ourselves about how it's made. Bees buzz from flower to flower to flower, using their long, tube-shaped tongues to suck up nectar. They bring the nectar back to the hive, where they regurgitate it into another bee's mouth. This process is repeated until the partially digested nectar is deposited into the honeycomb. The bees work together to fan the nectar with their wings until the water in it evaporates and they're left with honey. They then plug the honeycomb cell with a waxlike substance to store the honey—which humans harvest. Strangely, the National Honey Board has not invested millions of dollars into an advertising campaign reminding consumers: "It's sweet. It's delicious. It's bee vomit."

Oh, and one more thing. That shiny coating on your malted milk balls and Junior Mints? It also comes from bugs.

Shellac is used to give foods a waxy, shiny appearance. On food labels it may be identified as shellac or by any of these names: additive number 904, E904, lacca, gum lac, confectioner's glaze, pure food glaze, natural glaze, resinous glaze. Shellac enhances a product's appearance and provides a protective coating. It also helps keep moisture and oxygen out of products like candy, so they last longer. It can be found on candy corn, Milk Duds, Nestlé's Raisinets and Goobers, Sugar Babies, and jelly beans. It also is used to coat fresh fruit and vegetables, such as apples, pears, lemons, limes, oranges, cucumbers, bell peppers, and eggplants.

Shellac is not made from insects. Rather, it comes from excretions of the female lac insect. This parasite, scientifically known as *Kerria lacca* and *Laccifer lacca*, can be found in Asia, most often in the forests of India, Thailand, and Burma. The insects suck sap from banyan, soapberry, acacia, kusum, and fig trees. They then secrete a waxy, sticky substance called lac onto the twigs of the very trees where they've been feasting. When it's exposed to air, the lac hardens. The twigs become heavily encrusted in lac that is often an inch or more thick.

Lac harvest occurs twice per year. Farmers climb into trees to cut the resin-covered twigs from trees. Through a very labor-intensive and still-primitive process, the lac is crushed, melted off the twigs, refined, processed into resin flakes, and sold. Worldwide, more than 4 million pounds of lac are processed annually. Companies then dissolve the resin flakes in denatured alcohol to make liquid shellac.

Beyond food, shellac is used in all sorts of nonedible products, from paint and ink to fertilizer and floor polish. Lac bug secretions are also used in medicines, often as a coating that makes pills easier to swallow.

So the cold, hard truth is this: you end up eating insects and their by-products regardless of whether you intend to. Even if you avoid honey, grow and harvest your own grains, fruits, and vegetables, bake your own breads, and grind your own peanut butter, insect fragments will find a way into your food. They are unavoidable. And, as entomophagous folks around the world already know, they're actually pretty good for you.

FOOD	DEFECTS ALLOWED
Apple butter	Average of 5 or more whole or equivalent insects (not counting mites, aphids, thrips, or scale insects) per 100 grams of apple butter
Asparagus, fresh or frozen	10% by count of spears or pieces are infested with 6 or more attached asparagus beetle eggs and/or sacs OR Asparagus contains an average of 40 or more thrips per 100 grams OR Insects (whole or equivalent) of 3mm or longer have an average aggregate length of 7mm or longer per 100 grams of asparagus

FOOD	DEFECTS ALLOWED
Berries, canned or frozen (blackberries, raspberries, etc.)	Average of 4 or more larvae per 500 grams OR Average of 10 or more whole insects or equivalent per 500 grams (excluding thrips, aphids and mites)
Broccoli, frozen	Average of 60 or more aphids and/or thrips and/or mites per 100 grams
Cinnamon, ground	Average of 400 or more insect fragments per 50 grams
Chocolate	Average of 60 or more insect fragments per 100 grams when 6 100-gram subsamples are examined OR Any 1 subsample contains 90 or more insect fragments
Citrus juice, canned	5 or more Drosophila and other fly eggs per 250 ml or 1 or more maggots per 250 ml
Macaroni and noodle products	Average of 225 insect fragments or more per 225 grams in 6 or more subsamples
Mushrooms, canned or dried	Average of over 20 or more maggots of any size per 100 grams of drained mushrooms and proportionate liquid or 15 grams of dried mushrooms OR Average of 5 or more maggots 2 mm or longer per 100 grams of drained mushrooms and proportionate liquid or 15 grams of dried mushrooms

FOOD	DEFECTS ALLOWED
Peanut butter	Average of 30 or more insect fragments per 100 grams
Raisins, golden	10 or more whole or equivalent insects and 35 Drosophila eggs per 8 oz.
Tomato paste, pizza sauce, and other sauces	Average of 30 or more fly eggs per 100 grams, OR 15 or more fly eggs and 1 or more maggots per 100 grams, or OR 2 or more maggots per 100 grams in a minimum of 12 subsamples
Wheat flour	Average of 75 or more insect fragments per 50 grams

Source: FDA Food Defect Levels Handbook, May 1995; Revised March 1997 and May 1998. Content current as of September 2018.

8

Pass the Bugs, Please

If you're ever at a Seattle Mariners game at T-Mobile Park, you can snack on traditional baseball fare including popcorn, peanuts, hot-dogs, and chapulines.

Chapulines? Yes. The toasted grasshoppers are a popular snack at sporting events in Oaxaca, a region in southern Mexico, and they have been a hit at T-Mobile Park ever since they debuted in 2017. The insects, served in a chile-lime salt seasoning, often sell out. Each order contains roughly 40 grasshoppers. During the first two seasons, 2.8 million chapulines were purchased by fans. Whether they want an authentic Oaxacan dining experience, or they simply want to post videos of themselves eating big, crunchy bugs, the chapulines experiment has been an overwhelming success. In fact, in 2021, T-Mobile Park expanded its insect offerings by adding matcha ice cream with toffee-brittle mealworms to its menu.

Insects are not exactly commonplace on Western restaurant menus, but ballparks are hardly the only places you can find them.

Fazer Bakery is based in Finland and exports its products to 40 countries around the world. It started baking *sirkkaleipä*, an artisan bread made with cricket flour, in 2017. Bakan, an artsy, upscale Mexican restaurant in Miami, Florida, has two insect dishes on its menu: *guzanos de maguey*, pan-fried agave worms with guacamole and tortilla chips, and *escamoles*, ant eggs sauteed in butter, shallots, and herbs, served with guacamole and wrapped in a blue corn tortilla. In New York City, The Black Ant serves up grasshopper-crusted shrimp, chapuline tacos, and guacamole topped with black ant salt. The restaurant is also famous for its *croquetas de chapulín*, fried bundles made from yucca and grasshopper flours and a creamy white sauce, then garnished with roasted chapulines. In Montreal, Ta Chido features an appetizer-size serving of roasted grasshoppers, and at Market 707 in Toronto, diners can order Colombian-style empanadas filled with seasonal edible insects.

Roasted crickets and dried beetles still make their way into challenge baskets on high-profile TV cooking shows such as *Chopped*. But more and more chefs and home cooks are rising to the challenge and finding ways to include edible insects in dishes that are both delicious and visually appealing.

Kyle Fletcher, executive chef at Wye Hill Kitchen & Brewing in Raleigh, North Carolina, didn't have any experience working with edible insects when he agreed to compete in the North Carolina Museum of Natural Sciences' 2019 Critter Cook-Off. The competition is held as part of BugFest, an event that draws more than 35,000 visitors each year to see bugs, learn about bugs, and eat bugs. During the *Iron Chef*–style competition, he had 50 minutes to prepare an appetizer, entrée, and dessert using mealworms, superworms, crickets, and beetles.

"It was a cool experience," says Fletcher. "We got samples of the insects ahead of time so we could taste them and figure out the best ways to cook them. We tried them raw, then fried, and roasted. It was interesting to see how the different preparations brought out flavor complexities you wouldn't expect from a bug."[17]

Beetles proved to be the toughest culinary challenge for Fletcher. The insects are large with hard black shells. He toasted them to bring out their nutty flavor and then ground them up and made them into a spicy "beetle juice" that he served over yellowfin tuna and tempura-fried crickets as an appetizer. His entrée was flank steak stuffed with goat cheese and mealworm pesto, and dessert was cheesecake with a superworm and graham cracker crumb crust, topped with a beetle wing sugar shard. Fletcher's hard work and inventiveness paid off—he won the highly competitive cook-off.

Clockwise from the top: grasshoppers, ants, mealworms, and crickets.

"I'm not sure if the public is ready to consume insects on a regular basis," says Fletcher. "But they're sustainable and good for you, and if this experience taught me anything, they really can be made to taste pretty good."

You don't need to be a professional chef to begin experimenting with adding insects to your meals at home. Sprinkling whole roasted crickets into your granola or on top of your waffles is an easy way to get started. You can also make insects "disappear" into recipes by adding insect powder into everything from pizza dough to brownie batter.

It is important to note that many grains—including wheat, barley, and rye—contain a protein called gluten. When you bake, gluten helps hold foods together. Think of a pizza maker tossing dough into the air. Without gluten, the dough would easily crumble or tear. Cricket powder, however, does not have that sort of glutenous composition, so it won't bind batter or dough in the same way. When you bake with cricket powder, you cannot use it to replace all the flour in a recipe. A good rule of thumb is to use cricket powder to replace one quarter of the flour called for in a recipe. You can purchase premade mixtures of cricket flour to use in baking, or you can purchase cricket powder and blend it with wheat or other flours yourself.

Start experimenting with a favorite recipe. If your grandma's chocolate chip cookie recipe, for example, calls for two cups (250 g) of flour, try using one-and-a-half cups (188 g) of flour and a half a cup (62 g) of pure cricket powder. Mix and bake as usual. The dough may appear a little darker than usual, and it may taste a little nuttier. If you don't love the way the cookies taste, next time use just one quarter cup (31 g) of cricket protein instead. Every recipe is different, and people's tastes are different, so you may not get the ratio right the first time.

The recipes in this chapter are tried and true. They have been provided by this book's author, chefs, and people who work in the edible insect industry.

—————— KITCHEN SAFETY ——————

For successful cooking, be sure to read the recipe all the way through before you start. Assemble the ingredients and tools you'll need before you begin. Make certain your hair is pulled back, your sleeves are rolled up for most cooking (but down for frying to prevent splatter burns), and your hands are washed. Wear oven mitts when handling anything hot. Stoves, ovens, and sharp items, just as knives and graters, should only be used with adult supervision.

Edible Cookie Dough for Two

2 tbsp (28 g) unsalted butter, soft
1/4 cup (49 g) packed brown sugar
1/8 tsp (0.7 g) table salt
1/8 tsp (0.5 g) vanilla
1 tbsp (13 ml) milk
4 tbsp (25 g) all-purpose flour, heat treated*
1 tbsp (17 g) 100% cricket powder, mixed with flour prior to heat treatment
2 tbsp (20 g) chocolate chips

Mix together butter, brown sugar, salt, and vanilla until combined. Add milk and stir well. Slowly add heat-treated flour mixture, one tablespoon at a time, and stir well. Add chocolate chips; stir until combined. Refrigerate and enjoy chilled or eat the dough right away.
Recipe from Shelby Smith of Gym-N-Eat Crickets

* Flour comes from a grain that comes directly from the field; it is typically not treated to kill bacteria. When used in a product that's not baked, you can kill the bacteria yourself. Simply put the flour and cricket powder into a microwave-safe bowl. Microwave it on high for 1 minute and 15 seconds, stopping to stir every 15 seconds. Several companies are beginning to sell heat-treated flour as a specialty item. Be sure to read the label to keep yourself safe.

Peanut Butter Dip

1 cup (250 g) plain Greek yogurt
1/3 cup (95 g) creamy peanut butter
1 tbsp (21 g) honey
1 tbsp (17 g) 100% cricket powder
1 tsp (2.6 g) cinnamon or pumpkin spice

Place all ingredients in a small bowl. Blend with a hand mixer until smooth. Serve with apple slices, bananas, berries, or pretzels. Store in an air-tight container in the refrigerator.

Recipe from Shelby Smith of Gym-N-Eat Crickets

Actual Ants on a Log

2 celery stalks
1/4 cup (71 g)
   creamy peanut
   butter (or other
   nut butter)
2 tsp (1 g) roasted
   black ants

Rinse celery stalks. Trim ends and cut into 3- to 4-inch (7.5- to 10-cm) lengths. Spread peanut butter into the hollow of each stalk. Sprinkle roasted black ants over the top of the peanut butter. Enjoy!

Chocolate-Covered Crickets

1 cup (170 g) high-quality chocolate chips
1 cup (90 g) whole roasted crickets

Line a baking sheet with waxed paper or parchment paper. Set aside.

Place chocolate chips in a microwave-safe bowl. Microwave the chocolate 90 seconds, stopping every 30 seconds to stir the chocolate. Be aware that the bowl may become hot during the cooking process, so be careful while handling. If the chocolate is not completely melted, microwave in 15-second intervals, stirring between each interval until smooth.

Drop a roasted cricket into the chocolate and push it below the surface with a fork to coat. Use a fork to remove the cricket from the chocolate. Tap it gently against the side of the bowl until much of the chocolate has dripped off. Scrape the bottom of the fork on the edge of the bowl to remove excess chocolate. Slide the cricket onto the lined baking sheet. Repeat until you have coated all the crickets. Place the baking sheet in the refrigerator until the chocolate hardens, about 10 to 15 minutes. Remove chocolate crickets from the baking sheet and store in an air-tight container in the refrigerator. The crickets will keep for 7 to 10 days.

You can experiment with this recipe. Use milk chocolate or dark chocolate. Substitute roasted grasshoppers, or top with a sprinkle of sea salt or a drizzle of white chocolate.

Pineapple Banana Smoothie

1 frozen banana, cut into chunks
1/2 cup (83 g) frozen pineapple chunks
3/4 cup (184 g) almond milk
2 tbsp (34.1 g) 100% cricket powder
4 fresh mint leaves

In a blender, combine all ingredients. Pulse until smooth and mint leaves are fully blended. Pour into a serving glass. Enjoy!

Recipe from Charles Wilson of Cricket Flours

Avocado Toast with Mealworms

1 ripe avocado
Cricket salt or table salt and pepper, to taste
4 slices toast (your choice of bread)
4 tsp (2.2 g) roasted mealworms
Chia seeds (optional)

Place the avocado on a cutting board and cut it in half lengthwise, slicing into it until you feel the knife hit the pit, then rotate the avocado. Twist the avocado halves in opposite directions like you're turning two doorknobs, until they separate. Remove the pit with a spoon and discard it. Scoop out the flesh and put it in a bowl. Mash the avocado meat with a spoon or fork until slightly chunky. Season with desired spices, cricket salt, or plain salt and pepper. Toast the bread. Spread avocado mixture onto toast. Sprinkle with roasted mealworms. Garnish with chia seeds, if desired.

Recipe from Michela Dai Zovi, author of the cookbook Bugs for Beginners

Berry Beet Fruit Snacks

2 cups (380 g) fresh or frozen berries of your choice
1 small beet, steamed and skin removed
1/4 cup (59 ml) water
2 tbsp (43 g) honey (adjust amount to desired sweetness level)
2 tbsp (34 g) 100 % cricket powder
5 tbsp (46 g) unflavored gelatin

Line a 9-inch (22.9 cm) bread pan with parchment paper; spray paper with cooking spray.

Place berries and beets into a high-speed blender. Add water, honey, and cricket powder. Blend until smooth, at least five minutes. Taste the mixture; add additional honey if needed and blend again until smooth. Pour berry mixture into a large, heavy-bottomed pot. Sprinkle the gelatin evenly over the mixture. Do not touch for 5 minutes. When the mixture looks wrinkled on the surface, begin to whisk the gelatin into the fruit puree. Cook over medium heat while whisking constantly, until mixture is smooth. At first, the fruit mixture will appear clumpy, but the heat and whisking will smooth it. Do not let the mixture boil but cook until smooth.

Pour the mixture into the prepared bread pan and refrigerate for at least 3 to 4 hours or overnight. Once the mixture is set, use the parchment paper to lift it out of the pan. Use mini pie cutters to cut the set mixture into small fruit snacks with fun shapes. Use kitchen shears to cut any leftover scraps into more bite-sized pieces. The fruit snacks can be stored in an airtight container for about one week either at room temperature or in the refrigerator.

Recipe from Shelby Smith of Gym-N-Eat Crickets

Fluffy Bugana Bread

1/2 cup (113 g) unsalted butter
1 cup (200 g) granulated sugar
2 eggs
1 tsp (4.2 g) vanilla
2 small, ripe bananas, mashed*
1/2 cup (120 g) sour cream
1 1/4 cup (156 g) all-purpose flour
1/4 cup (137 g) 100% cricket powder
1 tsp (4.8 g) baking soda
1/2 tsp (3 g) salt
1/2 cup (59 g) chopped walnuts (optional)

Preheat oven to 350°F (177° C). Cream together butter, sugar, eggs, and vanilla. When combined, add bananas and sour cream. Mix on high speed for one minute. In a separate bowl, sift together flours, baking soda, and salt. Add butter mixture to the dry ingredients. Mix until well blended. If using nuts, add and mix well. Pour batter into 9-inch (22.9 cm) greased loaf pan. Bake for one hour or until

a toothpick inserted into the center comes out clean. Remove from oven and let bread cool in the pan for a few minutes. Then remove banana bread from the pan and let cool completely before serving.

*Banana bread is best made with bananas whose peels are speckled with brown or that have turned completely brown. These bananas are softer and sweeter and will give your bread a more intense banana flavor.

Chapulines

1/4 cup (57 g) avocado oil or vegetable oil
1/4 cup (52 g) onion, diced
1 serrano chile pepper, diced (stem and seeds removed)*
2 cloves garlic, lightly crushed
1 pound (454 g) chapulines (grasshoppers), legs and wings removed
    and discarded
1/2 tsp (2.8 g) table salt
1 lime

*When you handle serrano or any other hot peppers, you should wear some rubber gloves. The oils in the peppers can leave residue on your fingers and if you rub or your eyes, you'll feel an intense burning sensation. Carefully wash knives and cutting boards after you use them to make sure the residue does not transfer to the next food you chop.

Place the oil in a deep frying pan. When the oil is hot, add onions and chili pepper and saute. When the onions are soft and translucent, add the garlic and cook until everything is softened (about 1 minute more).

Remove the onions, chile pepper, and garlic from the oil with a metal slotted spoon and discard. Add the chapulines into the hot seasoned oil and stir occasionally, until they are nice and crispy. Remove chapulines from the oil and place on paper towels to absorb the oil. Immediately top with salt and squeeze a few lime wedges over them.

You can enjoy chapulines on their own, or you can eat them in a taco, topped with your favorite hot sauce, onions, and cilantro.

When cooked properly, chapulines are a deliciously salty, tangy, and crunchy snack. They can be hard to find, so if you come across any, grab them while you can.

Recipe from recipe developer Chelsie Kenyon

Cricket Protein Spicy Omelet

1 tbsp (13.6 g) extra virgin olive oil
1/4 to 1/2 Anaheim pepper, chopped
1 clove garlic, minced
1 shallot, chopped
1 to 2 tsp (5.7 to 11.4 g) 100% cricket powder
Pinch black pepper
Pinch fresh chopped parsley
3 eggs

Heat oil in a medium-sized frying pan. Add pepper, garlic, and shallot and cook over medium heat for 2 to 3 minutes or until softened. Set aside.

In a small bowl, mix together cricket powder, pepper, and parsley. Set aside. In another small bowl, lightly beat eggs. Slowly stir the eggs into the dry pepper/parsley/powder mixture.

Return medium frying pan to heat. Add egg mixture to cooked pepper mixture. Let the eggs cook for one minute, then use a heat-proof silicone spatula to gently lift the edges of the cooked eggs from the pan. Tilt the pan to allow the uncooked egg mixture to flow to the edges of the pan. Cook for 2 to 3 more minutes. Fold the omelet in half. Use a spatula to slide the omelet onto a plate.

Recipe from Charles Wilson of Cricket Flours

Cheddar Cricket Flour Biscuits

For Biscuits

1 1/2 cups (188 g) all-purpose flour
1/2 cup (137 g) cricket flour
1 tbsp (14.4 g) baking powder
1 tbsp (9.8 g) garlic powder
3/4 tsp (4.3 g) salt
1 tsp (2.3 g) smoked paprika
2 tsp (2.4 g) fresh parsley, chopped fine
1/2 cup (113 g) unsalted butter, melted
1 cup (225 g) buttermilk
1 cup (83 g) shredded cheddar cheese

For Topping

3 tbsp (42 g) unsalted butter, melted
1 tbsp (3.8 g) fresh parsley, chopped fine
1/2 tsp (1.6 g) garlic powder

Preheat oven to 450°F (232°C). Line a baking sheet with parchment paper; set aside.

In a large bowl, combine flours, baking powder, garlic powder, salt, paprika, and chopped parsley. In another bowl, whisk together butter and buttermilk. Pour buttermilk mixture over the dry ingredients and stir until just moist, being careful not to overmix. Gently fold in cheddar cheese.

Using a large spoon or quarter-cup measuring cup, scoop the batter evenly onto the prepared baking sheet. Bake for 10 to 12 minutes or until golden brown.

While biscuits are baking, whisk together topping ingredients in a small bowl. As soon as you take the biscuits out of the oven, brush their tops with the butter, parsley, and garlic powder mixture. Serve while warm.

Cricket-Coated Chicken Breasts

For the shake:

2 cups (180 g) roasted crickets, unseasoned
2 tbsp (36 g) salt
1/4 cup (56 g) Italian seasoning
4 cups (476 g) plain panko breadcrumbs
1 tbsp (13.6 g) vegetable or canola oil

For the bake:

4 medium-sized chicken breasts (may substitute pork chops)

Preheat oven to 350°F (177°C). Lightly grease a 9-by-13-inch (22.9-by-33-cm) baking dish.

Combine crickets, salt, and Italian seasoning in bowl of a food processor. Blend until fine. Add panko breadcrumbs and pulse a few times to combine all the ingredients.

Pat dry chicken breasts. Place meat in a large resealable plastic bag and add oil. Seal bag and massage to coat chicken in oil. Add breadcrumb mixture to the bag. Reseal and shake until coated.

Gently remove each chicken breast from the bag and place into prepared baking dish. Bake for 10 to 15 minutes or until chicken is no longer pink and juices run clear. (Baking time can vary greatly depending on thickness of meat.) Serve with mashed potatoes or rice. Garnish with some extra crickets for a nice little crunch.

Recipe from Executive Chef Kyle Fletcher, 2019 BugFest Cook-off Champion

Mini Cheesecake Cricket Protein Cups

Base

12 chocolate sandwich cookies
2 tbsp (28 g) unsalted butter, melted

Cheesecake

12 oz (336 g) cream cheese, softened at room temperature
1/2 cup (100 g) granulated sugar

1/2 cup (108 g) sour cream, room temperature
2 tsp (8.4 g) vanilla extract
1 tbsp (17 g) vanilla cricket protein powder
2 eggs, room temperature
5 chocolate sandwich cookies, crushed (for topping)

Preheat oven to 325°F (163°C). Line a muffin tin with 12 paper liners, set aside.

Remove the cream from the middle of 12 chocolate sandwich cookies. Seal the cookie wafers in a gallon-size plastic bag and crush using a rolling pin or the bottom of a cup; crush until only fine crumbs remain. Add melted butter to the crumbs and mix. Spoon the mixture into paper liners, about 1 tablespoon per cup. Press crumbs down firmly using the back of a clean, dry spoon. Bake chocolate bases for five minutes. Remove and cool.

Increase oven temperature to 350°F (177°C). Blend together the cream cheese and sugar using an electric mixer on low speed. Add sour cream and vanilla, blend again. Add cricket protein, blend again. Add both eggs to the mixture, beat once more until completely mixed and smooth. Crush four more chocolate sandwich cookies; gently stir the crumbs into the cheesecake mix. Spoon the mix into the paper liners on top of the chocolate base. Fill each liner three quarters of the way. Bake 10 minutes. Turn off the oven and leave the pan in the oven for 10 minutes longer.

Remove tin from the oven and allow to cool to room temperature before placing the cheesecake cups in the refrigerator to chill. Finely crush one more sandwich cookie; sprinkle crumbs over cheesecake cups before serving.

Recipe from Chirps

9

They're Not Just for Humans

If your dog is like most dogs, it likes treats. Perhaps it will sit for a treat. Shake for a treat. Lay down for a treat. Maybe it gets a treat when it comes inside and another at bedtime.

The American Kennel Club touts what it calls the "10 percent rule." Treats can make up to about 10 percent of your dog's diet. So, what if those treats were made from insect protein instead of salmon, chicken, duck, or beef? Suddenly your pet would be getting 10 percent of its protein from crickets or black soldier fly larvae.

And what if you were to replace Fido's old food with insect-based kibble? Suddenly your pet would be eating an all insect-based diet. That's Anne Carlson's hope.

Carlson is founder and chief executive officer of Jiminy's, an insect-based pet food company. She says pets are the perfect insect consumers because they don't overthink things. If something tastes good, they're going to eat it. (Jiminy's dog biscuits, for the record, look and smell like any other dog biscuit, and were devoured by this author's two Airedale terriers.)

Even after a consumer has decided to add insect-based products to their diet, Carlson says it's difficult to sell enough of those foods to make an environmental impact. "If I make an insect-based protein bar and it's absolutely delicious, someone may eat it once or twice a week," she says. "That's only about 7 percent of their eating occasions per week. Dogs and cats eat the same food and the same treats every meal, every day. If they're on an insect-based diet, you can capture 100 percent of their eating occasions. Now,

Cricket-based pet treats and foods are now commercially available.

we're talking about some real impact on our environment and sustainability."[18]

Jiminy's, based in Berkeley, California, entered the pet market with dog treats. In spring 2020, they launched their first insect-based dog foods: Cricket Crave, made with crickets, quinoa, and sweet potato, and Good Grub, made with dried black soldier fly larvae, oats, and sweet potato. Researchers say switching just one dog from a chicken-based diet to an all insect-based diet could save as much as 480,000 gallons (1.8 million l) of water per year. If all the nearly 90 million dogs in the United States switched to insect-based food, water savings would be upward of 43 trillion gallons (163 trillion l). That's enough to fill the Great Salt Lake 10 times and still have water left over.

A study done by researchers at the University of California, Los Angeles, suggests that dogs and cats account for 25 percent to 30 percent of the environmental impacts from all animal production in the United States. That figures in water, fossil fuel, pesticides, and more. That impact is significant, but that doesn't mean the path to getting insect-based pet foods on the market has been an easy one.

The US Food and Drug Administration works alongside the Association of American Feed Control Officials to review and approve pet food ingredients. The approval process can take years and requires all sorts of documentation showing that an ingredient is safe and beneficial. Because there isn't a lot of scientific research out there regarding edible insects for pets, Carlson has hired scientists to conduct experiments regarding the digestibility of various insects in pet food. While waiting for official approval on the insects, she convinced regulators to certify her pet food as GRAS (generally recognized as safe). With this preliminary certification in hand, Carlson began selling her products both online and through retailers such as Petco and Mud Bay. Dog-related products came first, cat treats and food are on their way.

Jiminy's certainly isn't the only insect-based pet food company, but there really aren't many. EnviroFlight, based in Yellow Springs,

Ohio; Chippin in Takoma Park, Maryland; Enterra Feed of Langley, British Columbia; and Wilder Harrier in Montreal, Canada, are notable pioneers. Yora Pet Foods in Great Britain and France's Ynsect are also making waves in the market. For now, the cost of insect-based foods from these and other companies is about four times the cost of budget pet foods, and on par with luxury brands.

Do you think the big, traditional pet food companies are paying attention to this movement? They are.

Mars Petcare, the world's largest pet food manufacturer, makes more than 50 brands, including Pedigree, Whiskas, IAMS, and Royal Canin. Dr. Jo Gale, senior manager of global science advocacy, told Veterinary Information Network in early 2020, "While the industry is in its early stages, we believe that exploring these types of alternative ingredients and technologies could allow us to work to improve the future of pet nutrition."[19]

Nestlé Purina PetCare is another industry giant, making brands including Purina Pro Plan, Purina Dog Chow, Friskies, and Beneful. The company began testing a line of pet food made with cricket protein in 2019 under the brand name RootLab. "Issues like overfishing, over-farmed land, invasive species and millions of tons of greenhouse gas emissions from livestock are all on our radar," the company states on its website. "We strive to use ingredients whose nutrition is currently untapped, and healthy proteins that have a far smaller impact on the environment than traditional ingredients."[20]

Meanwhile, veterinarians around the world are wrestling with questions about the safety and nutritional value of insects. The American Veterinary Medical Association has taken no official stance on insect-based foods. They are choosing, instead, to wait for the completion of feeding trials that show the diet is safe in the long term. The British Veterinary Association, on the other hand, has suggested that some insect-based foods would be both a healthier and more environmentally friendly alternative to meat-based pet foods. In an August 2019 interview with BBC News, Simon Doherty, the group's president, said, "There's a really exciting future for the use of insect protein for companion animals. It's a fantastic opportunity—looking at insects to provide alternative sources of some of the nutrient ingredients we use in pet food diets."[21]

Insect diets already are being fed on North American fish and poultry farms. Aquaculture is the farming of fish, crustaceans, mollusks, and other organisms. Worldwide, more fish are farmed than are caught wild. Farmed fish have traditionally been fed fishmeal, plant-based feeds, and oil from fish and plants. Fishmeal, used to feed fish, poultry, and hogs, is produced from wild fish caught in the oceans. In 2020, aquaculture consumed an estimated 10 percent of the world's fish production as food for other fish.

The rising cost of fishmeal and fish oil, along with concerns about overharvesting, have meant more and more farmers have been relying on plant-based feeds. Turns out, most fish cannot stomach that sort of diet. In their search for suitable replacements, researchers have found that insect meal—often black soldier fly or mealworm—is a good substitute.

Free-range chickens often eat insects, scratching and pecking in search of dinner. In 2018, dried black soldier fly larvae received the FDA's stamp of approval as an ingredient in commercial poultry feed. A team of researchers from the United States and Korea explored the use of black soldier fly larvae as feed for broiler chicks. The 2018 study found that the insect-based diets boosted chicks' weight, as well as their ability to fight off disease.

Governmental reviews are underway in the United States regarding the use of insects as feed for hogs, even as research into the practice continues. The notion has support. As the world's appetite for meat grows, some scientists say insects could provide the nourishment livestock need at a lower environmental cost. Some of the most promising feeder insects can be raised on diets of manure, food waste, and grains discarded by breweries, which gives them an even bigger environmental boost. When talking about insects that humans are already consuming themselves, some are left wondering: *If I can eat it, why can't a pig?*

Others insist on going slow and taking the time to weigh the benefits against potential safety risks. Is it possible insects could pass along toxins or diseases to farm animals that eat them? Is it possible those animals could pass on the poisons and diseases to humans? There are reports of allergic reactions in humans after eating insects. Could those same reactions occur in farm animals?

Insects as feed may be the gateway to getting people to consider insects as food, says Jiminy's Carlson. "We're talking about the future of the planet here," she says. "Insects are a sustainable solution. They are a humane solution. But, it's more than that. They're delicious and nutritious. Maybe feeding them to livestock or to our best friends can be a first step."[22]

10

DIY Cricket Farming

If you have a garden or even a container of herbs on your kitchen counter, you probably know the pride that goes along with growing your own food. Knowing how and where your food was grown magically seems to make it taste better. Homegrown tomatoes are juicer, carrots are crunchier, and strawberries are sweeter.

Unfortunately, unless you live on a farm, raising your own livestock is probably out of the question. Many cities and towns have rules about what types of animals you can raise in your yard, and most neighbors probably wouldn't be too excited about nonstop mooing, oinking, or cock-a-doodle-doing—not to mention the manure. Pee-ew!

Ah, but raising insects is something you can do in even the smallest of spaces. Mealworms and ants are quieter, but this DIY tutorial focuses on crickets because they're the most commonly farmed insect in North America.

Becoming an at-home cricket farmer takes an investment of under $80, less if you can use recycled totes, screens, pie tins, containers, or other materials you already have on hand. Caring for the little buggers requires some real dedication and may make for a fun family project.

Think you're up to the challenge? Here is a list of the supplies you will need to get started:

* 2 20-gallon (75.7 l) plastic totes with lids
* 2 feet x 2 feet (0.2 m x 0.2 m) piece of aluminum window screen
* 8-quart (5.6 l) bag of perlite
* 2 pie tins
* 8-quart (5.6 l) bag of organic potting soil
* 6 small plastic containers, each about 1-inch (2.54 cm) deep
* 4 sponges, cut to fit into the small plastic containers
* Misting bottle
* 2 heat lamps
* 2 thermometers
* 6 empty, clean cardboard egg cartons
* 50 to 100 live crickets
* Food scraps: fruits, vegetables, leafy greens, cooked pasta
* Hot glue gun

Before you bring any crickets home, you will want to spend some time getting their new homes—the plastic totes—ready. To allow for ventilation, cut a hole about 6 inches in diameter into the end of each tote. Cut the window screen into pieces large enough to cover these holes; use hot glue to hold the screens in place. Baby crickets are really tiny. It's smart to use a double layer of screen crisscrossed one on top of the other to lessen the chance of escape.

Use a damp cloth or paper towel to wipe off the inside of the tote; you don't want any chemical residue lingering in there. The smooth interior walls of the tote will keep the crickets from climbing out.

Next, spread a layer of perlite in the bottom of each tote. Perlite is the stuff in potting soil that looks like tiny Styrofoam balls. It is made from naturally occurring compounds found in soil and contains no toxic chemicals. Perlite can retain some water while

A screened hole in your tote will provide ventilation.

allowing the rest to drain away. That's important, because crickets thrive in a moist environment.

Fill the two pie tins with damp potting soil. This is where the female crickets will lay their eggs. Nestle the pie tins into the perlite at one end of each tote. Place saturated sponges into four of the plastic containers. Place two of those containers in each tote, nestling them into the perlite near the soil. Place a third, empty plastic container in each tote—this will be where you place the crickets' feed. You can purchase special cricket feed, or you can feed your orchestra (the name for a group of crickets) a variety of fruits, vegetables, greens, and pasta. Focus on using food scraps that would otherwise be headed to the compost bin: potato or carrot peels, bruised apple slices, leftover lettuce. Try to vary what you are feeding your crickets to keep them happy and healthy.

Fill the remaining space in the tote with loosely stacked cardboard egg cartons. These cartons create dark, cozy spaces in which the crickets can live. Place a thermometer in the lower portion of each tote and hang a heat lamp above the totes to boost the temperature. Crickets like it warm. You'll want to do periodic checks

Empty egg cartons provide hiding places for the crickets.

to ensure you're keeping the inside of the totes between 80 and 90 degrees Fahrenheit (26°C–32°C). Some heat lamps have temperature controls. If yours doesn't, you can adjust the temperature the old-fashioned way: make it warmer by lowering the lamp and cooler by raising it further from the tote. Heat lamps can pose a safety risk if not used properly. Keep all flammable materials away and make certain they are securely fastened so they can't fall.

Once your cricket "farm" is set up, it is time to add your crickets. Starter crickets are easier to find than you might imagine. The *Acheta domesticus* and *Gryllodes sigillatus* varieties are most often raised for human consumption, but other species are perfectly safe to eat. Many pet stores sell them as feed for reptiles and amphibians. You can buy a box of 50 to 100, or order from an online source. Once you buy your starter crickets, your farm should become self-sustaining.

Ideally, you'll want to buy crickets that are approximately one-quarter inch (64 mm) long. Those crickets are about a week old

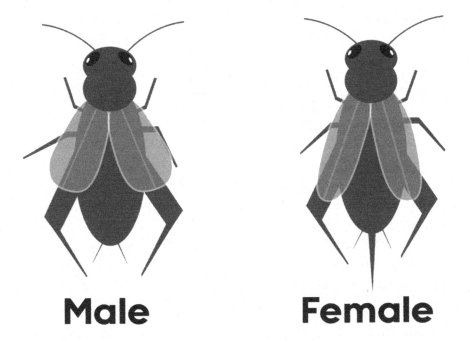

Male   **Female**

and will have time to get used to their new environment before they begin laying eggs. Do not fill your cricket farm with crickets you catch in the wild; there's just no way to know if those insects have come into contact with harmful chemicals.

It is important to have a mix of male and female crickets—preferably more female than male. How can you tell the difference? Female crickets have three long extrusions on their behinds. The main one, called the ovipositor, is used to deposit eggs into the soil. Male crickets have two extrusions. Another difference: Female crickets have large wings. Male crickets have smaller, paddle-shaped wings that are used to create the insect's familiar chirping sound.

Your first batch of crickets will all go into one tote. Make sure the two sponges in this tote are wet, but there's no more than one-quarter inch (64 mm) of water in each container; this will prevent accidental cricket drownings. Place fresh food in the food dish. Place your crickets in the lower part of the tote. Use the spray bottle to mist the inside of the tote and quickly put the lid on the tote.

Caring for your crickets isn't difficult, but they do require daily attention. At least once each day you need to replenish their water supply and switch out their food so it doesn't spoil. You may be tempted to leave uneaten food in the bin for an extra day, but don't. The warm temperatures will cause it to spoil and it will get stinky or, worse, make your crickets sick. Check the thermometer to make sure the temperature inside the tote is warm enough, and mist the inside of the tote, focusing on the soil. Once eggs are laid in the soil, it must be moist for them to hatch.

As you start your cricket farming operation, it's a good idea to keep a log of what's happening each day. Start with a simple notebook where you record the date, temperature, what time you changed water and feed, and other notes. This would be a good place to jot down questions, observations, and concerns. Did you feed your crickets something they especially loved? Are your crickets especially sleepy or energetic? You'll also want to make note of when you begin to see the first cricket eggs.

Date	Temp AM	Water	Food	Mist	Temp PM	Notes
June 1	83	10:00 AM	10:00 AM	10:00 AM	85	
June 2	87	8:30 AM	8:30 AM	8:30 AM	86	Chirping started
June 3	84	9:45 AM	9:45 AM	10:30 AM	90	
June 4	92	10:00 AM	10:00 AM	10:00 AM	90	20+ dead in water bowl
June 5	89	7:45 AM	8:00 AM	7:45 AM	97	

When the environment within the tote is optimal, the male crickets in your orchestra will begin to chirp by scraping their wings together. This is called stridulation, and it is their way of showing off for the female crickets. Researchers believe females choose their mates based on the pitch and tempo of the chirps. Soon after the chirping begins, female crickets will use their ovipositors to begin laying eggs in the pans of soil. Cricket eggs look like very tiny grains of rice. Each female cricket will lay up to 200 eggs. After 8 to 10 days, the pan will be filled with eggs. At this point, you need to remove the pan of soil from the first tote and place it in the second tote.

Now, for a short period, you will have two totes to monitor. Make sure both are warm and that you're misting them at least once each day. After about a week, baby crickets, called nymphs, will begin to hatch. They will break out of the egg capsule and dig their way out of the dirt. When the first nymphs appear, you'll need to provide them with food and water. Baby crickets drown very easily. Use only a damp sponge with no excess water in the container, or quartered potatoes, to water your nymphs.

Nymphs look like small versions of adult crickets with a few differences: the babies don't have wings until they're about a month old and the females do not have ovipositors. As they grow, the nymphs will shed their hard exoskeletons through a process called molting. New exoskeletons are light gray and soft, making the molted crickets vulnerable. Luckily, the new exoskeletons begin to harden within just a few hours. A cricket will molt eight to ten times during its lifetime.

Crickets reach maturity at six to eight weeks. If you're raising the crickets to feed to an amphibian or reptile, you can feed them live and at nearly any point throughout their life cycle. If you're harvesting them to feed yourself or to make treats for a pet, you'll need to freeze them. The low temperatures put the crickets into a deep state of hibernation from which they never wake up. Getting the crickets into the freezer can be tricky—especially the first go-round. If you have a freezer large enough to hold the entire tote, you can place it inside for two to four hours. After they freeze, you can collect the dead crickets into plastic bags.

You can also place the egg cartons, covered with crickets, into large, resealable bags. Those bags can be placed in the freezer. Another option is to work over the tote to shake crickets from the cartons into your plastic bags. Again, those bags must be placed in the freezer.

Crickets should be treated the same way you'd treat any other raw food. It's best to keep the crickets frozen until you're ready to use them. Food safety experts recommend prepping them by boiling a pot of water, placing the crickets in a wire mesh strainer, and then rinsing the crickets with a steady stream of boiling water. This process is called blanching.

The blanched crickets can be enjoyed right away, or you can roast them. At this point, you will need an adult helper. To roast, cover a baking sheet with parchment paper. Place the crickets onto the prepared baking sheet in a single layer and roast for 3 to 4 hours in a 200°F (93°C) oven. If you want to eat the crickets as a snack, this is a good time to season them with salt, pepper, or other spices. If you're planning to make your crickets into cricket powder, there's no need to season at this point. Roasted crickets are delicate and lightweight. You can grind them in a food processor or coffee grinder. It takes about 1,000 roasted crickets to make one pound of cricket powder.

After each harvest, you need to work to prepare the newly available tote to hold your next litter of crickets. Clean the tote and replace the perlite. Fill the pie tin with fresh soil. Wash the food and water containers and trade the old sponges for new ones. When the tote of baby crickets starts chirping, place a pan of dirt in it so they can lay eggs and continue the cycle.

Raising crickets is not without risk. You may lose crickets because they drown, or if you can't get the temperature or humidity just right. If bins get too full or you're not properly caring for them, crickets can begin eating each other. Family members or neighbors may complain about the chirping or smell. And until you become comfortable opening and closing the totes, it's likely you'll have some escapees.

But the process also comes with rewards. It is a great hands-on science experiment that allows you to sharpen your investigative and observation skills. It provides an up-close look at what cricket farmers must do every day and allows you to think about what parts of the process could be automated or simplified. And, best of all, a successful harvest will leave you with some high-protein snacks that, because you raised them yourself, will be even tastier.

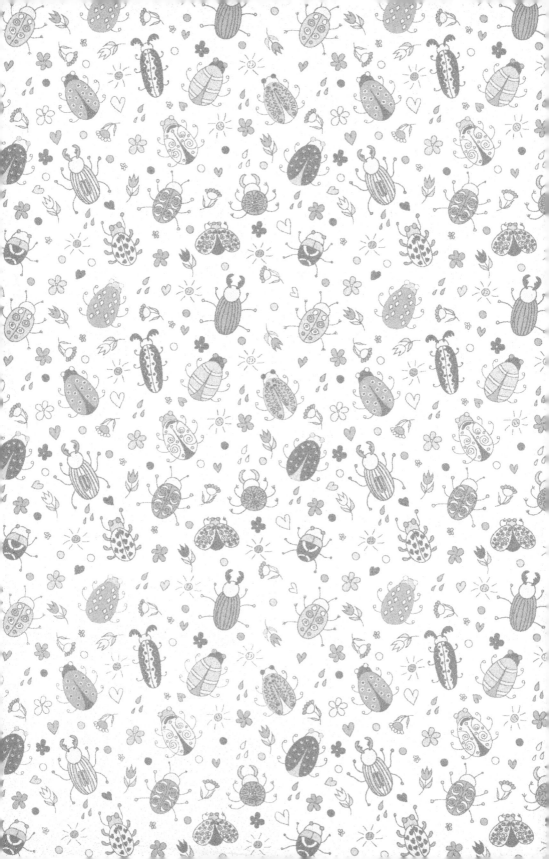

11

Can Insects Fix Food Supply Problems?

If you visited a supermarket during the COVID-19 pandemic, you likely saw empty refrigerator cases where meat, milk, and eggs were supposed to be. Shelves that once held flour, yeast, beans, pasta, and rice were bare.

Shoppers were panicked. Families that previously stopped by McDonald's on the way home from soccer practice or celebrated the end of each week with dinner at their favorite pizzeria were suddenly eating breakfast, lunch, and dinner in their own homes. Schools closed and so did school lunchrooms. Many adults started working from home, so they no longer ate lunches out with their coworkers. More meals needed to be eaten at home, which meant more groceries would be needed.

Meanwhile, around the world, crops rotted in fields because laborers were not allowed to work, or they were scared they might catch the virus if they did work. Meat processing plants in Iowa, Minnesota, and South Dakota were shut down because of COVID-19 outbreaks among workers. Tyson Foods, one of the world's largest food companies, produces nearly one-fifth of the beef, pork, and chicken in the United States. It sells more than two dozen food brands including Jimmy Dean, Hillshire, Ball-park, and Sara Lee. In spring 2020, Tyson was hit with lowered demand from restaurants and corporate clients as governments enforced social distancing rules. Suddenly, there were no profes-sional sporting events selling concessions. There were no amuse-ment parks entertaining thousands of families each day. There were no business conferences. The 60-count packages of hot dogs, for instance, that they would have sold to restaurants weren't needed, but they couldn't easily be repackaged to be sold in supermarkets where they were needed. Facilities were forced to shut down, and temporary meat shortages plagued grocery stores across the country.

Major supermarket chains such as Kroger, Giant Eagle, Weg-man's, and Costco put purchase limits on some products, meat included. One-fifth of the Wendy's restaurants in the United States stopped selling burgers and other beef products.

At the same time, farmers in North America and Europe were forced to dump milk and eggs because demand from schools, hotels, restaurants, and coffee shops plummeted during lockdown. Trans-portation restrictions made it difficult to bring products to market. Florida farmers threw away thousands of pounds of zucchini, cab-bage, and tomatoes. Squash rotted in California fields. Idaho farm-ers dug huge ditches to bury millions of onions.

To make matters even worse, some countries implemented bans (most of them short term) on food exports, to make sure they could feed their own people. Kazakhstan, for instance, banned the exportation of flour and wheat. India stopped exporting rice. Cam-bodia stopped exporting fish and rice.

Increased demand, lower production, fewer imports, plus delays in distribution added up to higher prices for groceries. From March 2020—the month most of North America began to go on lock-down—to May 2020, market research firm Nielsen found a nearly 6 percent spike in food prices. Millions who already struggled to feed their families were suddenly in an even more dire situation. Food banks were there to help, but many who needed assistance were forced to line up for miles in their cars, waiting for food give-aways. Feeding America, the United States' largest hunger relief organization, reported 60 percent more people were turning to food banks in June 2020 compared to the year before.

Experts say there wasn't necessarily a food shortage, but the people who needed food often could not get it or couldn't afford it if they could find it. That's a supply chain problem. Supply chain is the term that describes how food gets from a farm to your table. Each step along the way is like a link of chain: one each for the farmer, processor, distributor, retailer, and consumer. If something goes wrong with one of those links, the whole chain is affected. The global pandemic didn't cause permanent damage to the world's food supply chain, but it proved how fragile it is.

Our food supply chain has been dinged before. Natural disasters and extreme weather events present challenges. Hurricanes, tornadoes, wildfires, and earthquakes can damage roads and railways, making it difficult to get food supplies into an area. Storms can destroy supplies that already are on hand. And they can have long-lasting effects. In 2018, when Hurricane Florence hit southeastern North Carolina, 6,000 hogs were killed. Beyond the obvious loss of animals, a handful of manure pits were damaged, allowing pollution to flow into nearby rivers, lakes, and streams. Those contaminated waterways had to be cleaned to reduce the risk of contaminating other animals and crops.

Climate change has wreaked havoc on the world's food supply, as have chemical spills and airborne pathogens such as bird flu, swine flu, and SARS.

Why is all this important in a book about edible insects? Because these food-supply challenges have everyone trying to figure out how to ensure food shortages don't happen again. How can we make certain everyone has food when and where they need it? Bugs, it seems, may be part of the solution.

Marion Gross, chief supply chair officer for North America at McDonald's says the COVID-19 crisis has revealed a need for a more "agile, diverse supply chain."[23] Ideally, that would include a variety of suppliers, from local farmers to global agriculture companies.

Foods made with cricket flour can bridge the gap when other protein sources aren't available.

By increasing the diversity of foods and food sources available, the risk associated with any one of those foods or food sources decreases. Crickets, mealworms, and black soldier fly larvae certainly add to the world's food diversity. Research conducted by a team of five Korean scientists was published in the August 2019 edition of the journal *Food Science of Animal Resources*. It concluded: "Using insects can potentially solve problems related to the conventional food-supply chain, including global water, land, and energy deficits."[24]

Making edible insects more widely available adds another healthy protein option for consumers, and not just during a pandemic. Beef or turkey are suddenly unavailable? No problem, you could get your protein by eating bread or waffles made with cricket flour.

Insects can contribute to food security with less environmental impact than many other foods. They can help strengthen the world's food supply chain.

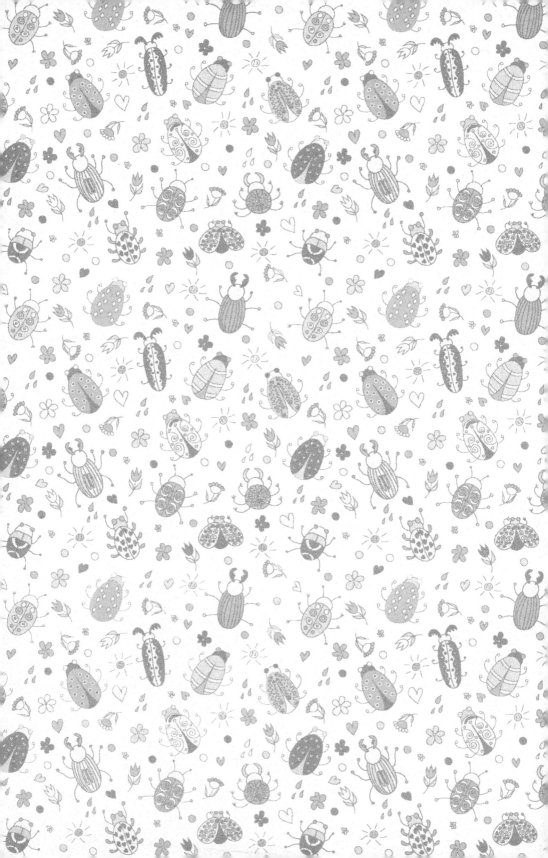

12

Your Questions Answered

The idea of eating insects is new to a lot of people. New things naturally prompt questions. The purpose of this chapter is to anticipate and answer some of your most common entomophagy and entomology questions.

WHAT DO INSECTS TASTE LIKE?

That's kind of like asking, "What does fruit taste like?" Lemons, bananas, and watermelons are all fruit, but their flavors and textures are very different. The same goes for insects.

Even within a specific species of insect, the way each tastes can vary depending upon what the insect has been fed and the environment in which it was raised. Preparation also plays a huge role in flavor. In general, whole roasted crickets taste like toasted sunflower seeds or walnuts, and cricket powder adds a nutty flavor to baked goods.

Black ants have a lemony taste. Mealworms, which are actually beetle larvae, have the texture of tiny cheese puffs and a mild, slightly nutty flavor. Dragonfly larvae and other aquatic insects taste like fish, cockroaches taste like mushrooms, red agave worms are spicy, and striped shield bugs have an apple-like flavor. Grasshoppers are wildly crunchy with a mild chicken flavor, and wasps taste like pine nuts.

IS EATING INSECTS DANGEROUS?

It is possible that insects that aren't raised in sanitary conditions could pose health threats. Insects harvested from the wild may be contaminated by pesticides, or perhaps they've eaten food scraps contaminated with fungus or disease-causing bacteria.

As with any food, you should know where the insects you're eating came from. Additionally, insects' exoskeletons are made of chitin, similar to what is found in crustaceans, such as crabs, lobsters, and shrimp. If you're allergic to shellfish, there is a good chance you may be allergic to insects.

CAN YOU EAT RAW BUGS?

In many countries, insects are consumed not only raw but alive.

That can present health risks. Insects (much like meat) can contain parasites. Cooking can kill those parasites—along with dangerous bacteria. So, cooking insects is a good idea. It also minimizes the "yuck" factor of squishy bug guts.

CAN I EAT THE SAME CRICKETS I BUY AT THE PET STORE?

While they're alive, crickets being raised as animal feed and those raised for humans are treated exactly the same. So, as long as you're buying live insects to process yourself, you're probably OK.

Once crickets die and become a food product, those intended for human consumption need to be treated the same way as any other food. Cricket farmers must comply with the same safe handling, labeling, and packaging regulations as someone producing vegetables or fruit.

WHEN I EAT A CRICKET, DO I EAT THE WHOLE CRICKET?

That's up to you. Some people pull off the legs but, after eating a few, most don't bother with that. And, when cricket powder is made, it's made from whole crickets—no limbs or organs or anything else removed.

Now, just because you're eating it, that doesn't mean it's digestible. Researchers estimate about 20 percent of a cricket cannot be digested by humans. Remember that chitin is insoluble fiber, but it still provides a benefit by helping move things through your digestive system. About 80 percent of a cricket is considered edible and digestible, compared with 55 percent for chicken and pigs, and about 40 percent for beef cattle.

ARE THERE BUG-EATING COMPETITIONS?

There are some insect-eating competitions, but they are much, much lower profile than the hot dog– or chicken wing–eating contests you might see on television. Some museums and festivals hold informal bug-eating competitions to draw attention to the practice of entomophagy.

The Schiele Museum of Natural History in Gastonia, North Carolina, for example, hosts an annual bug-eating competition as part of its Bug Day. The ten-round showdown has ten participants gobbling insects ranging from dung beetles to zebra tarantulas. The contestant with the slowest eating time each round is eliminated, until a champion is crowned.

The Chinese city of Lijiang also hosts an annual bug-eating contest. Contestants dressed in traditional garments attempt to gobble down as many bugs as they can in five minutes. How many bugs are we talking about? The 2017 winner ate an impressive 2.71 pounds (1.23 kg) of bamboo worms.

You probably should not set up your own bug-eating competition. Doctors warn that the risk of choking is high, whether you're wolfing down doughnuts or darkling beetles.

DO INSECTS FEEL PAIN WHEN THEY'RE KILLED?

Scientists are not certain about whether insects feel pain or, if they do, how much pain they feel. Researchers from the University of Queensland in Brisbane, Australia, researched this topic and found no evidence of "an insect showing protective behavior towards injured body parts, such as by limping after leg injury or declining to feed or mate because of general abdominal injuries."[25] In fact, they found insects continuing normal activities even after severe injury or after body parts had been removed. At the same time, they thought that some insect behavior, such as struggling when sprayed with insecticide, could be a response to pain, or it could simply be a reflex.

Until more research can be done, the Food and Agriculture Organization of the United Nations suggests that, as a precaution, farmed insects should be killed using methods that reduce suffering. It recommends freezing or instantaneous techniques, such as shredding. Placing insects in a container in the freezer causes them to enter a state called diapause, a deep sleep much like hibernation. The temperatures are then lowered even more, and the insects die.

WHAT IS THE BEST WAY TO START EATING INSECTS?

That's up to the individual. If you are someone who likes trying new things, you might jump right in by mixing in some whole roasted crickets with your popcorn, or by crunching on a handful of spiced grasshoppers.

But, if you're like most people, you might want to start a little slower. What's a food you love? You can add cricket powder to lots of everyday

Roasted crickets on popcorn.

foods and get started that way. Put a little cricket powder in your milkshake or pancake batter. You'll be an entomophage before you know it.

WHAT IF YOU JUST CAN'T STAND SEEING THEIR LITTLE HEADS WHEN YOU EAT THEM?

Well, there's insect powder. That's 100 percent pure insects, but ground into a fine dust. No visible heads, legs, or antennae.

Another alternative: scientists in at Wageningen University in the Netherlands have been experimenting with growing cells from silkworms and gypsy moths in large containers of liquid. It's a type of biotechnology that produces insect cells but no actual insects. Those cells could be used to develop medicines, fabrics, and other products—even food—for human use. It's still in the experimental stage, but it remains a possibility that you could someday eat bugs without actually eating bugs.

HAS EATING INSECTS EVER REALLY SAVED SOMEONE'S LIFE?

Yes, insects provide much-needed nutrition to many malnourished people in developing countries. But those aren't the only lives they've saved.

In August 2020, Minnesota teacher Jonathan Ceplecha was cutting down trees with a chainsaw when a tree fell, and he was pinned underneath. Both his legs were broken and he had no way to call for help. Ceplecha was trapped for four days before rescuers found him. He survived by eating plants and insects and drinking rainwater. His story is not that unusual. Backpacking, outdoor, and survival publications often share information about edible insects and plants.

US military manuals say insects should be eaten when other food sources are not available. And that's not just talk. In 1996, Air Force captain Scott O'Grady's plane was shot down over Bosnia. He parachuted into enemy territory and hid from enemy forces for nearly a week, eating little more than ants and drinking rainwater.

The problem many folks face is that once they find themselves stranded in the wilderness, they don't know which insects are safe to eat and which aren't. The advice survival experts offer is this: stay clear of brightly colored insects and ones that smell bad. Of course, there are exceptions to this rule, but it's better to be safe than sorry.

SHOULD WE WORRY THAT EATING TOO MANY INSECTS WILL MAKE THEM GO EXTINCT?

Insects are an important part of many ecosystems. They aerate the soil, pollinate blossoms, and nourish birds, reptiles, amphibians, and fish. They feed on dead plants and animals, helping to return nutrients to the soil.

About 40 percent of all insect species are at risk of extinction because of habitat loss, pollution, and climate change. Insect farming doesn't have much of an effect on insect populations, but harvesting wild insects does. In central Zimbabwe, for example, mopane trees were once covered with mopane worms. Because the worms were overharvested for decades, the harvests are now significantly lower.

Few countries have any sort of regulations preventing overharvesting of wild insects. Rules or guidelines could help protect at-risk wild insects.

WHERE CAN YOU BUY EDIBLE BUGS?

If insects are being raised and processed near where you live, it is possible you'll be able to find them at a farmer's market or your local supermarket. Some health food stores carry insect-based protein bars and chips. Many insect farmers sell their products online. You can also find crickets on the menu at a handful of upscale restaurants across the country; you might also look for them at your local Mexican, Vietnamese, or Thai restaurant.

13

Will My Bug Diet Really Make a Difference?

There are 7.7 billion people in the world. There are 579 million people just in North America. So, it is perfectly fair to ask: can one person eating insects make any kind of difference in terms of sustainability, impact to the environment, or ending world hunger?

The answer is yes.

First of all, the change in your diet and your health and the shrinking of your carbon footprint are all notable on their own. An average person needs about 1.8 ounces (50 g) of protein per day. If you ate protein from insects one day per week, you could save about 42,927 gallons (162,500 l) of water in a year. By yourself.

But there is also what's known as the ripple effect. The act of adding cricket powder to your smoothie once a week is like dropping a pebble into a body of water. After the initial plop and splash, ripples spread out, carrying energy as they go. Just as the ripple effect continues spreading the pebble's impact, the changes you make may encourage others to do the same. Pretty soon, instead of just one cricket smoothie being consumed at your breakfast table, your dad and brother want one too. Your best friend sees you snack on roasted mealworms at lunch and asks if you can pack some for her to try too. Your soccer teammates see how much more energy you have during workouts and they ask their parents to let them try edible insects. Pretty soon your teammates' parents want to give them a try. Then their coworkers and those coworkers' families.

We're not talking about instant radical change. It's unlikely your consumption of insects will suddenly make them more popular than popcorn at movie theater concession stands. But the ripples you start by eating insects can have widespread and long-lasting effects.

The difference you make can be even more impactful and reach a broader audience if you intentionally set out to tell others about edible insects. Below are some ideas to get you started.

SCIENCE FAIR EXHIBIT

Many schools host annual science fairs, where students conduct experiments and share findings on everything from growing crystals to testing for lead in drinking fountain water. There are lots of experiment possibilities associated with edible insects. Start with a question you have about entomophagy:

* Are boys or girls more willing to taste bugs?
* Are adults or kids more likely to try bugs?
* What's the most cricket protein I can add to a smoothie before it becomes gross?
* Are people more willing to eat snakes or insects?
* Are people more willing to eat whole roasted crickets or cricket cookies?
* Do crickets fed only vegetables taste different than crickets fed only fruit?

Next, think of a possible answer, called a hypothesis, and use experiments to test if your hypothesis is true.

Most science fairs require you to create a poster or display explaining your experiment. It's a great way to share information.

RESEARCH PROJECT

The next time your teacher assigns a research project or speech and says it can be on any topic, perhaps that topic should be entomophagy. Read books, watch videos, interview cricket farmers, tour an edible insect farm. Learn all you can. This is a double win, because it means you get to dig deep into a subject that interests you, and you can share that knowledge with your classmates.

TASTE TEST

Who doesn't like to be asked what they think about different foods?

A taste test event allows participants to sample foods they might not otherwise try. Hold the event at school, church, or at a club meeting. Just be sure you have the permission and support of your teacher or leader. Perhaps you may even want to run a taste test at your next family gathering.

Successful tasting events usually focus on no more than four food items. Tasting too many items at once can be confusing for tasters. Comparing similar items is often easiest. For example, you could purchase two different kinds of chocolate protein bars: one made with cricket protein and one made with whey. Cut the bars into bite-size chunks and see if tasters can tell which bar is which. Or pass out samples of roasted crickets, mealworms, ants, and beetles. Ask tasters what they think about the smell, appearance, texture, and taste of each of the edible insects.

Remember, whenever you offer edible insects to someone, you need to let them know that they may be allergic if they have a shellfish allergy.

TEST RECIPES

Test kitchens are places where new recipes are developed, fine-tuned, and written so others can make the same dish at home.

Large companies in the food industry have them, as do cooking magazines, food-oriented TV shows, and recipe developers.

You can set up your own personal test kitchen where you experiment with edible insect recipes. Maybe you want to see how mealworms could be incorporated into your dad's lasagna, and then analyze the nutritional value of your new recipe. Take lots of notes about the new recipe's smell, taste, and appearance.

Be sure to give your recipes fun insect-related names. Chop tomatoes, basil, garlic, and roasted crickets to create a new take on bruschetta called "bugschetta." Replace the chocolate chips in a cookie recipe with roasted crickets to create chocolate "chirp" cookies. Or, perhaps you want to give yourself a challenge to come up with the best possible dessert using beetles.

Not every dish will be a success, but if you learn from your not-so-great experiments, you'll ultimately come up with some recipes worth sharing.

COOKING PARTY

Once you've got some insect-based dishes you're comfortable making, invite some friends or family over to help you cook. While you're chopping and stirring, you can share some fun facts about entomophagy. If you get really ambitious, you could plan a meal that features insects in every dish. Your friends can help prepare and enjoy the food when it's finished.

If an entire meal is too much, invite your friends over to bake brownies made with cricket flour. Or challenge a group of friends to make insect-based toppings for ice cream sundaes. Get creative!

USE TECHNOLOGY

If computers are your thing, you could build a website showcasing all the things you know about edible insects. Post recipes, links to articles, and pictures. Start a blog. Make it as fancy or simple as you want.

Social media is another fantastic place to catch people's attention. Snap and share photos of your cricket-eating adventures. Run online surveys. Ask your friends: "Would You Eat This?"

One person eating crickets won't make a huge difference, but you can make *a* difference. Sometimes that's as small as getting people to open their minds to what's possible.

Liz Camacho is chief operating officer of Chirps, a cricket-based snack food company that won financial backing from American entrepreneur and investor Mark Cuban when they appeared on the show *Shark Tank*. She says she takes every opportunity she gets to talk to people about edible insects. And, yes, it's part of her job, but this goes on way after work hours. "Every time I wear my EAT BIGS shirt, I prove that I'm a walking, breathing, real person who eats insects. Even if I don't say a word, I'm making people think," Camacho says. "If someone in the supermarket or at a school event asks me a question, I never give them the hard sell. I'm not asking them to never eat a hamburger again. I am asking them to consider—just consider—instead of eating ten hamburgers in a month, maybe eating eight or nine and looking at a more sustainable protein for that extra meal or two."[26]

Baby steps. Small changes that can be sparked by one taste, one conversation, one article or poster or presentation.

So, back to the original question: can one person eating insects make any kind of difference in terms of sustainability, impact to the environment, and ending world hunger?

Yes, they absolutely, one hundred percent can. One ripple at a time.

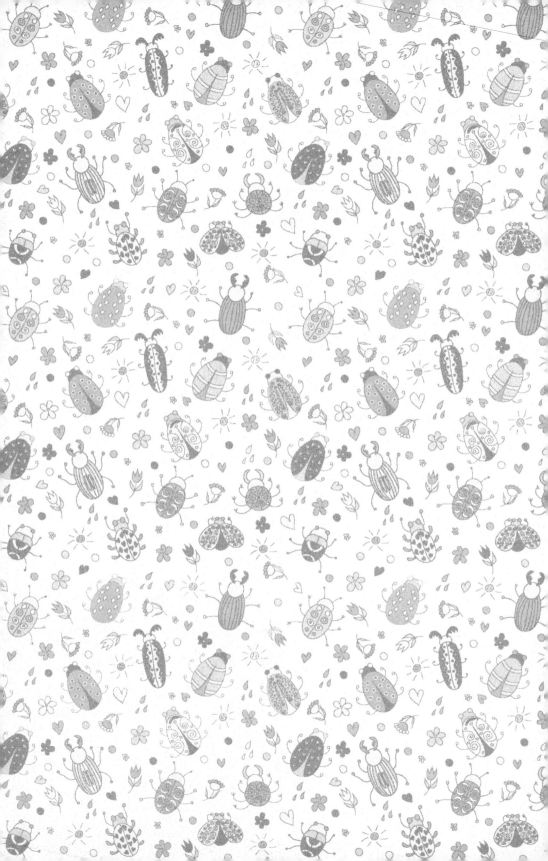

Acknowledgments

This book has only come to life because of the incredible support I have received along the way. Thanks to my agent, Stacey Kondla, for her unwavering belief in this project, and to my editor, Jerome Pohlen, a true master of wordsmithing. Thanks also to my critique group members: Adria, Annie, Dalton, Elizabeth, Jeanne, Jeff, Jennifer, both Jessicas, Joe, Karen, Larry, Lisa, Margaret, Paula, Sandra, Shannon, Shelley, Stephanie, and Wendy—who all read countless versions of these chapters over the past few years. I am forever grateful for the support and knowledge I've received from them and from others in the Society of Children's Book Writers and Illustrators.

Thanks, too, to the many people within the edible insect industry who answered my never-ending stream of questions. Shelby Smith of Gym-N-Eat Crickets is a cricket-farming goddess.

The amazing teachers I had as a kid growing up in Manchester, Iowa, fostered my love of reading and research. Thanks to Karen Flora, Janice Grundmeyer, Kathy and Lee Rempe, Helen Schmidt, Velma Swanson, and others for fueling my curiosity.

My husband and kids became taste-testers as I experimented with cricket recipes and they humored me as I routinely shared insect-related facts at the dinner table. Mitch, Eve, and Eli, you are my world.

Last, thanks to my parents Dean and Sue Boone, my sister Bev Beevers, and my brother Doug Boone for their steadfast love and encouragement.

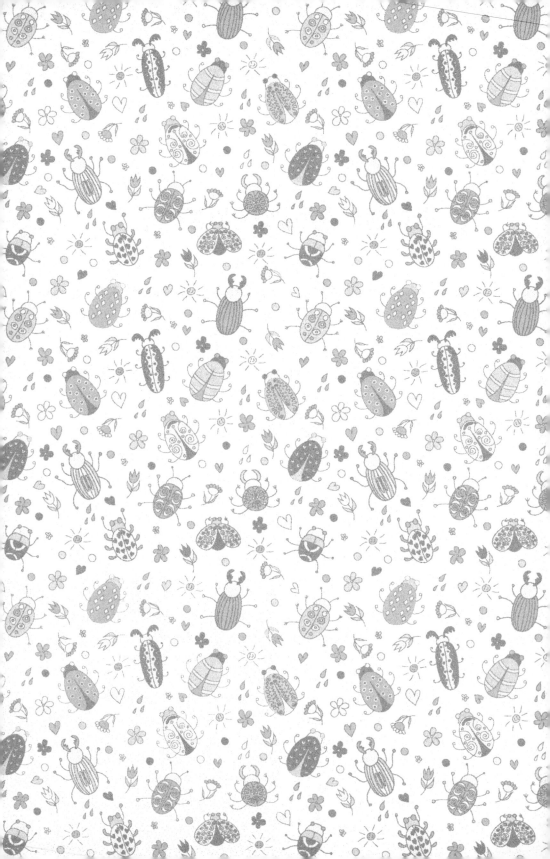

Notes

"If you don't eat insects": Julie J. Lesnik, interview by author, July 5, 2018.

"I think the future of food": Loulla-Mae Eleftheriou-Smith, "Insurgent Style Shailene Woodley: 'I Think the Future of Food is Insects," Independent, March 27, 2015, www.independent.co.uk.

"Instead of them eating our vegetables,": Naseh Shaker, "When Life Gives You Locusts: Yemenis Turn a Plague Into Dinner During Ramadam," Middle East Eye, June 2, 2019, www.middleeasteye.net.

"My dad's been a farmer most of his life" through *"The ventilation, the temperature, the watering"*: Shelby Smith, interview by author, July 31, 2019.

"I was training with a group" through *"I'm not one to force these things on anybody,"*: Tammy Mann, interview by author, July 16, 2020.

"Good nutrition is important to young people": Lisa Lovejoy, interview by author, September 22, 2020.

"People in the industry always talk about": John Galt, "Ethical Considerations and Nutritional Benefits of Insects in a Plant-Based Diet," presentation given at the North American Coalition for Insect Agriculture's Eating Insects Athens conference, August 13, 2018.

"I doubt insects fart" through *"Because of their anatomy"*: Aram Mikaelyan, interview by author, August 11, 2020.

"Growing up, our family always had" through *"For a lot of people, it comes down to"*: Charles Wilson, interview by author, July 17, 2020.

"We simply don't have the money": Cheryl Preyer, interview by author, October 16, 2020.

"an abnormal and persistent fear of insects": Ayşegül Taylan Ozkan and Kosta Y Mumcuoğlu, "Entomofobi ve Deluzyonel Parazitoz" [Entomophobia and delusional parasitosis], *Turkiye parazitolojii dergisi* 32, no. 4 (2008): 366–70.

"While the emotion is universal": Disgusting Food Museum website, https://disgustingfoodmuseum.com.

"Our aim is to open people's minds": What a Museum of Disgusting Food Reveals About Human Nature," January 19, 2020, www.economist.com.

"For most people, if they haven't eaten a bug": Cheryl Preyer, interview by author, October 16, 2020.

"Have been established because": US Food and Drug Administration Department of Guidance and Regulation, Food Defects Handbook, www.fda.gov.

"Farms and processing plants are clean": Jeff Nelken, interview by author, August 3, 2020.

"While it is a safe product": Nancy Shute, "Is That a Crushed Bug in Your Frothy Starbucks Drink?," NPR, March 30, 2012, www.npr.org.

"It was a cool experience" through *"I'm not sure if the public is ready"*: Kyle Fletcher, interview by author, August 14, 2020.

"If I make an insect-based protein bar": Anne Carlson, interview by author, July 15, 2020.

"While the industry is in its early stages": Ros Kelly, "There's a Fly in My Kibble! Insect-Based Pet Food Takes Off," Veterinary Information Network News Service, March 16, 2020, https://news.vin.com.

"Issues like overfishing, over-farmed land": "Purina Tests New Food Brand Made with Crickets and Carp Protein," Pet Product News, March 11, 2019, www.petproductnews.com.

"There's a really exciting future": Roger Harrabin, "Insect-Based Food 'Better for Pets than Top Steak,'" BBC News, August 27, 2017, www.bbc.com.

"We're talking about the future of the planet": Anne Carlson, interview by author, July 15, 2020.

"Agile, diverse supply chain": "North America's Food Supply Chain: Disruption, Adaptation and Evolution," Food Service Consultant, Publication of Food Service Consultants Society International, August 14, 2020, http://www.fcsi.org.

"Using insects can potentially solve problems": Tae-Kyung Kim, Hae In Yong, Young-Boong Kim, Hyun-Wook Kim, Yun-Sang Choi, "Edible Insects as a Protein Source: A Review of Public Perception, Processing Technology, and Research Trends," *Food Science of Animal Resources*, August 2019.

"An insect showing protective behavior": C. H. Eisemann, W. K. Jorgensen, D. J. Merritt, M. J. Rice, B. W. Cribb, P. D. Webb, and M. P. Zalucki, "Do Insects Feel Pain? – A Biological View," *Cellular and Molecular Life Sciences*, February 1984.

"Every time I wear my EAT BUGS shirt": Liz Camacho, interview by author, July 14, 2020.

Sources

I started casually researching the topic of entomophagy in 2013, when the United Nations first issued its report about the possibility of using edible insects to feed the world's growing population. I was intrigued, but the notion seemed far off and far away.

Soon after, I got a chance to travel to Vietnam and Cambodia on a two-week trip with my daughter. I had promised myself I would be open to new experiences along the way. Biting into a fried grasshopper the size of my thumb in a crowded market in Hanoi was a very new experience. The taste was not memorable, but the crunch? Years later, I still remember chewing and chewing, almost as if I were eating shrimp shells.

At first, I put this insect-eating experience into a "novelty" category, along with the time I sampled chocolate-covered ants or had seen spiders encased in colorful lollipops. It was the kind of thing you would try once so you could brag to your friends about it.

Before long, though, I began to gain a better understanding of insects as food. I learned there are many places in the world where people have long eaten insects, and I was introduced to an enthusiastic group of scientists, farmers, chefs, and sustainability experts who are promoting their consumption in North America. Along the way, I have perfected the art of baking with cricket flour, adding it to everything from pizza dough to chocolate chip cookies. Do we eat insect-based products at every meal? No. But I can definitely see their potential.

Biting into that crispy, crunchy grasshopper changed my thinking. These sources provided the information necessary to bring this story to life.

INTERVIEWS

Kevin Bachhuber, North American Coalition for Insect Agriculture. September 17, 2020.

Geert Boelen, founder of One Hop Shop. July 31, 2019.

Liz Camacho, CEO of Chirps Chips. July 14, 2020.

Anne Carlson, founder and CEO of Jiminy's. July 15, 2020.

Kyle Fletcher, executive chef at Wye Hill Kitchen and Brewery, Raleigh, North Carolina, and 2019 BugFest Critter Cook-Off champion. August 14, 2020.

Chelsie Kenyon, recipe developer specializing in Mexican cuisine. September 28, 2020.

Julie J. Lesnik, assistant professor of anthropology at Wayne State University. July 5, 2018.

Lisa Lovejoy, sports/wellness dietitian. September 22, 2020.

Tammy Mann, founder of Harmony Cricket Farm. July 16, 2020.

Aram Mikaelyan, assistant professor of entomology and plant pathology at North Carolina State University. August 11, 2020.

Aly Moore, Bugible blogger. February 26, 2019.

Jeff Nelken, BS, MA, Food Safety & Accident Prevention Training. August 3, 2020.

Cheryl Preyer, North American Coalition for Insect Agriculture. October 16, 2020.

Shelby Smith, founder of Gym-N-Eat Crickets. July 31, 2019.

Charles Wilson, founder and CEO of Cricket Flours. July 17, 2020.

Annie Zeimis, One Hop Shop CFO. July 31, 2019.

BIBLIOGRAPHY

I did a lot of research of current articles and scientific reports on this topic. A full research bibliography can be found at www.boonewrites.com. Direct quotes are cited in the notes, and below I've included a bibliography of books and guides that may be of special interest to young readers.

D'Asaro, Laura, Rose Wang, and Heather Alexander. *Project Startup #1: Eat Bugs*. London, England: Penguin Workshop, 2021.

Dai Zovi, Michaela. *Bugs for Beginners: The Most Complete Guide to Teach You How to Cook Edible Insects*. Seattle: KDP Publishing, 2018.

Gates, Stefan. *Insects: An Edible Field Guide*. London, England: Ebury Press, 2018.

Gordon, David G., Chugrad McAndrews, and Karen Luke Fildes. *The Eat-a-Bug Cookbook: 40 Ways to Cook Crickets, Grasshoppers, Ants, Water Bugs, Spiders, Centipedes, and Their Kin*. Berkeley, CA: Ten Speed Press, 2013.

Grace Communications. "The Water Footprint of Food." Water Footprint Calculator. April 25, 2020. www.watercalculator.org /footprint/foods-big-water-footprint/.

Huis, Arnold van, Henk van Gurp, and Marcel Dicke. *The Insect Cookbook: Food for a Sustainable Planet*. New York: Columbia University Press, 2014.

Lesnik, Julie J. *Edible Insects and Human Evolution*. Gainesville: University Press of Florida, 2019.

Lockwood, Jeffrey Alan. *The Infested Mind: Why Humans Fear, Loathe, and Love Insects*. New York: Oxford University Press, 2013.

Menzel, Peter, and Faith D'Aluisio. *Man Eating Bugs: The Art and Science of Eating Insects*. Berkeley, CA: Ten Speed Press, 1998.

US Food & Drug Administration, Department of Guidance and Regulation. *Food Defect Levels Handbook*. May 1995; revised March 1997 and May 1998. Source correction February 2005.

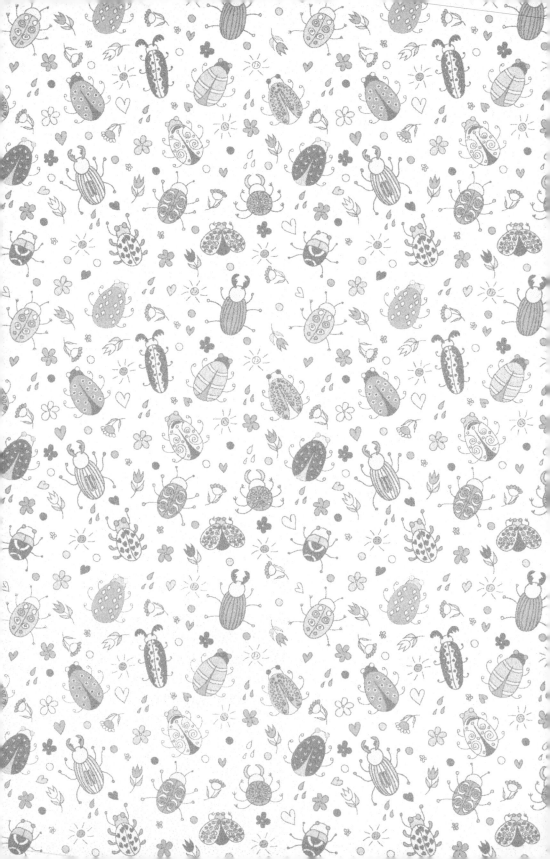

Index

Entries in italics refer to images; entries in bold refer to recipes